Biography of Gospel Song and
Hymn Writers

AMS PRESS
NEW YORK

Yours Sincerely
J. H. Hall.

Biography of Gospel Song and Hymn Writers

By
J. H. HALL

FULLY ILLUSTRATED

NEW YORK   CHICAGO   TORONTO

Fleming H. Revell Company

LONDON   AND   EDINBURGH

Reprinted with special persmission of the
Fleming H. Revell Company

Reprinted from the edition of 1914, New York
First AMS EDITION published 1971
Manufactured in the United States of America

International Standard Book Number: 0-404-07226-7

Library of Congress Number: 70-144626

AMS PRESS INC.
NEW YORK, N.Y. 10003

To

*all gospel song and hymn writers ; to
all singers and lovers of gospel song ;
this book of biography is with appreciation dedicated by the author*

To hide true worth from public view,
Is burying diamonds in their mine,
All is not gold that shines, 'tis true;
But all that is gold ought to shine.

—Bishop.

Preface

WHILE books of biography of men and women in different vocations of life are numerous, including not a few biographical volumes of the old Master Musicians, the present volume is, so far as the author is aware, the first distinctive book of biography to be published of the men and women whose gospel songs and hymns have thrilled the hearts of innumerable hosts, and kindled the fire of the great evangelistic movement all over the world.

The author found that to insert all the worthy names of gospel song and hymn writers in a single volume would make it too bulky ; it is hoped it may be possible to follow this work with a second volume. Beginning with Dr. Lowell Mason, the writer has endeavored to give a sketch and portrait of leading representatives of gospel song and hymn writers up to the present time. It is but natural that people should wish to know something of the lives, and be pleased to see the portraits of the composers whose songs and hymns have brought joy, peace and comfort to their hearts. It is confidently anticipated that the reading of these brief sketches will add new life and power to the gospel in song.

The author feels that in a measure Mr. J. H. Fillmore has made this volume of biography possible, by granting permission to use a number of sketches

11

published in *The Musical Messenger*, issued by the Fillmore Bros., Cincinnati, O., and to whom he offers his most sincere appreciation. Credit is due the *Musical Million* for the sketch of the author. He also wishes to thank all who in any way assisted in securing data, etc., in the preparation of these sketches. Such a work required labor and patience, but if these sketches give interest and pleasure, and a higher conception and appreciation of the beauty and power in gospel song, the author will feel abundantly rewarded.

J. H. H.

Dayton, Va.

Contents

CONTENTS

DR. LOWELL MASON.

I

Dr. Lowell Mason

D R. LOWELL MASON (the degree was conferred by the University of New York) is justly called the father of American church music; and by his labors were founded the germinating principles of national musical intelligence and knowledge, which afforded a soil upon which all higher musical culture has been founded. To him we owe some of our best ideas in religious church music, elementary musical education, music in the schools, the popularization of classical chorus singing, and the art of teaching music upon the Inductive or Pestalozzian plan. More than that, we owe him no small share of the respect which the profession of music enjoys at the present time as contrasted with the contempt in which it was held a century or more ago. In fact, the entire art of music, as now understood and practiced in America, has derived advantage from the work of this great man.

Lowell Mason was born in Medfield, Mass., January 8, 1792. From childhood he had manifested an intense love for music, and had devoted all his spare time and effort to improving himself according to such opportunities as were available to him. At the age of twenty he found himself filling a clerkship in a banking house in Savannah, Ga. Here he lost no opportunity of gratifying his passion for musical advancement, and was fortunate to meet for the first time a thoroughly qualified instructor, in the person of F. L. Abel. Applying his spare hours assiduously to the cultivation of the pursuit to which his passion inclined him, he soon acquired a proficiency that enabled him to enter the field of original composition, and his first work of this kind was embodied in the compilation of a collection of church music, which contained many of his own compositions. The manuscript was offered unavailingly to publishers in Philadelphia and in Boston. Fortunately for our musical advancement it finally secured the attention of the Boston Handel and Haydn Society, and by its committee was submitted to Dr. G. K. Jackson, the severest critic in Boston. Dr. Jackson approved most heartily of the work, and added a few of his own compositions to it. Thus enlarged, it was finally published in 1822 as The Handel and Haydn Society Collection of Church Music. Mason's name was omitted from the publication at his own request, which he thus explains :—

" I was then a bank officer in Savannah, and did not wish to be known as a musical man, as I had not the least thought of ever making music a profession." President Winchester, of the Handel and Haydn Society, sold the copyright for the young man. Mr. Mason went back to Savannah with probably $500 in his pocket as the preliminary result of his Boston visit.

The book soon sprang into universal popularity, being at once adopted by the singing schools of New England, and through this means entering into the church choirs, to whom it opened up a higher field of harmonic beauty. Its career of success ran through some seventeen editions. On realizing this success,

Mason determined to accept an invitation to come to
Boston and enter upon a musical career. This was in
1826. He was made an honorary member of the
Handel and Haydn Society, but declined to accept
this, and entered the ranks as an active member. He
had been invited to come to Boston by President Winchester and other musical friends and was guaranteed
an income of $2,000 a year. He was also appointed,
by the influence of these friends, director of music at
the Hanover, Green, and Park Street churches, to al-
ternate six months with each congregation. Finally he
made a permanent arrangement with the Bowdoin
Street Church, and gave up the guarantee, but again
friendly influence stepped in and procured for him the
position of teller at the American Bank.

In 1827 Lowell Mason became president and conductor of the Handel and Haydn Society. It was the
beginning of a career that was to win for him as has
been already stated the title of " The Father of American Church Music." Although this may seem rather a
bold claim it is not too much under the circumstances.
Mr. Mason might have been in the average ranks of
musicianship had he lived in Europe ; in America he
was well in advance of his surroundings. It was not
too high praise (in spite of Mason's very simple style)
when Dr. Jackson wrote of his song collection : " It is
much the best book I have seen published in this country, and I do not hesitate to give it my most decided
approbation," or that the great contrapuntist, Hauptmann, should say the harmonies of the tunes were
dignified and churchlike and that the counterpoint was
good, plain, singable and melodious.

Charles C. Perkins gives a few of the reasons why

Lowell Mason was the very man to lead American music as it then existed. He says:

" First and foremost, he was not so very much superior to the members as to be unreasonably impatient at their shortcomings. Second, he was a born teacher, who, by hard work, had fitted himself to give instruction in singing. Third, he was one of themselves, a plain, self-made man, who could understand them and be understood of them."

The personality of Dr. Mason was of great use to the art and appreciation of music in this country. He was of strong mind, dignified manners, sensitive, yet sweet and engaging.

Prof. Horace Mann, one of the great educators of that day, said he would walk fifty miles to see and hear Mr. Mason teach if he could not otherwise have that advantage.

Dr. Mason visited a number of the music schools in Europe, studied their methods, and incorporated the best things in his own work. He founded the Boston Academy of Music. The aim of this institution was to reach the masses and introduce music into the public schools. Dr. Mason resided in Boston from 1826 to 1851, when he removed to New York. Not only Boston benefited directly by this enthusiastic teacher's instruction, but he was constantly travelling to other societies in distant cities and helping their work. He had a notable class at North Reading, Mass., and he went in his later years as far as Rochester, where he trained a chorus of five hundred voices, many of them teachers, and some of them coming long distances to study under him. Before 1840 he had developed his idea of " Teachers' Conventions," and, as in these he had representatives from different states, he made musical missionaries for almost the entire country. He left behind him no less than fifty volumes of musical collections, instruction books, and manuals.

As a composer of solid, enduring church music, Dr. Mason was one of the most successful this country has produced. He was a deeply pious man, and was a communicant of the Presbyterian Church. Dr. Mason in 1817 married Miss Abigail Gregory, of Leesborough, Mass. The family consisted of four sons, Daniel Gregory, Lowell, William and Henry. The two former founded the publishing house of Mason Bros., dissolved by the death of the former in 1869. Lowell and Henry were the founders of the great organ manufactory of Mason & Hamlin. Dr. William Mason was one of the most eminent musicians that America has yet produced.

Dr. Lowell Mason died at " Silverspring," a beautiful residence on the side of Orange Mountain, New Jersey, August 11, 1872, bequeathing his great musical library, much of which had been collected abroad, to Yale College.

> He died full of years and of honor,
> For honor lies in honest toil.

W. B. BRADBURY.

II

William B. Bradbury

THE churchgoing people of to-day are generally familiar with the name Wm. B. Bradbury. Many have cherished that name from childhood. Most of us began our musical experiences by singing his songs, and as early experiences are the most lasting, we will carry these melodies, with their happy associations, through life.

Mr. Bradbury, in his day, created a style of juvenile music, especially Sunday-school music, that swept the country. He set the pattern for his successors in Sunday-school song-making, and those who have harped on the key-note that he struck have been most successful. True, we have improved some in the way of hymns, and a smoother voicing of the parts, but there are still many Sunday-school song writers who regard Mr. Bradbury's writings as the ideal.

William Batchelder Bradbury was born at York, York County, Maine, October 6, 1816. He came of a good family. He spent the first few years of his life on his father's farm, and rainy days would be spent in the shoe-shop, as was the general custom in those days. He loved music, and would spend his spare hours in studying and practicing such music as he could find. In 1830 his parents removed to Boston, where he saw and heard for the first time a piano and organ, as well as various other instruments. The effect was to lead him to devote his life to the service of music. Accordingly he took lessons upon the organ, and as early as 1834 had achieved some reputation as an organist.

He attended Dr. Mason's singing classes, and later was admitted into his celebrated Bowdoin Street church choir, and the Doctor proved to be a valuable and steadfast friend.

After some months he was asked to preside at the organ of a certain church at a salary of twenty-five dollars per annum. On trying the organ he found it to be one of those ancient affairs which required the keys to be *pulled up* as well as pressed down, and he suggested that his pay should be at least fifty dollars, since the playing required this double duty. It was not long till a better paying situation was offered him—that of one hundred dollars a year.

At the age of twenty he was still singing in Dr. Mason's choir, when one evening at recess, the Doctor laid his hand on his shoulder, and said: "William, I have an application for a teacher at Machias, Maine, to teach three large singing schools, besides private pupils, and I believe you are just the man for the place." He was overjoyed and delighted. He sent his terms, which were accepted, and achieved success. After a busy year and a half of work at Machias, he returned to Boston to marry his sweetheart, and then located at St. Johns, New Brunswick. Here the people did not take sufficient interest in his work, and he returned to Boston. Then came a call to take charge of the music of the First Baptist Church of Brooklyn. Dr. Mason gave him a letter of introduction.

At the time of his taking charge of the organ at the Brooklyn church there was some opposition to the organ among the members. He being aware of it took pains to play it so well, and in such good taste, that he speedily won all to favor its use.

After a year's work here the important era in his career began. He took charge of the choir and organ of the Baptist Tabernacle, New York City, and in addition started a singing class for the young.

This first class was visited by many superintendents and others interested in Sunday-schools, who were uniformly delighted with what they saw and heard, and the originator of the movement soon found himself engaged in many similar schools in various parts of the city. These classes became very popular. In the Spring Street Church there was a class of over six hundred. From these schools sprang the celebrated "Juvenile Musical Festivals," as they were called, held at the Broadway Tabernacle, which, for some years, were such a prominent feature among the musical events of the city. Those annual concerts were occasions never to be forgotten by any who were present.

The sight itself was a thrilling one. A thousand children were seated on a gradually rising platform, which spread the scene, as it were, most gracefully before the eye. About two-thirds of the class were girls, dressed uniformly in white with a white wreath and blue sash. The boys were dressed in jackets with collars turned over, something in the Byron style. When all were ready, a chord was struck on the piano—a thousand children instantly arose, presenting a sight that can be far more easily imagined than described. Of the musical effect produced by such a chorus we will not attempt to speak.

Mr. Bradbury improved every occasion of these large

gatherings to impress upon the public the necessity of musical instruction in the public schools, and in time he had the satisfaction of seeing music taught as a regular study in the public schools of New York.

While he was teaching among the children, he would occasionally compose a song for them, and to their delight. So he decided to make a book. " The Young Choir " was the result. This was in 1841. Being an inexperienced writer, he got Dr. Hastings to correct his music. The book was a success, and others followed.

Mr. Bradbury had a desire to go to Europe and study with some of the masters there, and on the second day of July, 1847, he took passage for England, accompanied by his wife and daughter. They were thirty days on the ocean. He remained in London some weeks, and made good use of his time while there. He made the acquaintance of Jenny Lind, then quite unknown to American fame.

He arrived in Leipsic, Germany, September 11th, where he made arrangements to begin his studies without delay. Wenzel was his teacher for the piano and organ ; Boehme for voice ; and Hauptmann for harmony. This city was the home of Mendelssohn, whose death occurred only a few weeks after Mr. Bradbury's arrival, and whose funeral he had the sad privilege of attending.

It need scarcely be stated that Mr. Bradbury pursued his studies with the greatest assiduity.

While thus zealously devoting himself to personal cultivation and improvement, Mr. Bradbury was in no danger of losing sight of the work at home for which he was preparing himself. He visited many public and private schools, and familiarized himself thoroughly with all the German methods of popular musical instruction. He also made the acquaintance of many prominent musicians. He made a short but very interesting tour across the Alps into Switzerland. After his return to New York, in 1849, he devoted his entire time to teaching, conducting conventions, composing, and editing music books. In 1854, in connection with his brother, E. G. Bradbury, he commenced the manufacture of the Bradbury pianos, which at one time were quite popular.

Prof. Wm. B. Bradbury was one of the great trio (the other two being Drs. Mason and Root) to which the church and vocal music of this country owe much. Mr. Bradbury was an excellent composer. His melodies have an easy, natural flow, and his harmonies are simple and natural, and many of his hymn-tunes and gospel songs still in use are among the best that American writers have produced. He was unceasingly active, having edited fifty-nine books of sacred and secular music, a large part of which were his own work.

Professor Bradbury was an excellent conductor and teacher. He was always kind, patient, and full of sympathy for others. Mr. Bradbury died at his residence, Montclair, N. J., January 8, 1868, leaving a widow, four daughters and a son. He will always occupy a prominent place in American musical history.

DR. GEO. F. ROOT.

III

Dr. George F. Root

THE subject of our sketch was the product of that period in our national life in which the parents devoted themselves preëminently to training their children to habits of industry, and to teaching them the strictest morality and religion. Inheriting a strong physical constitution, and starting out from a typical New England home a pure boy with high aspirations, he attained the highest place among American musicians as a teacher, a theorist and composer.

George Frederick Root was born in Sheffield, Mass., August 30, 1820. His father moved to North Reading, near Boston, when the boy was six years old, and there his youth was spent.

He was always fond of music—not singing at all as a boy, but played upon every kind of instrument that came in his way. At thirteen it was his pride that he could "play a tune" on as many instruments as he was years old. His dream of life was to be a musician, although such an ambition was looked down upon by all his relatives and friends, excepting a fond mother.

In the fall of 1838 he went to Boston and made an engagement to work for Mr. A. N. Johnson and take lessons on the piano.

His father and one of the brothers were at the time in South America, and the mother, with six younger children, was at home on the farm. When he secured

the engagement with Mr. Johnson to receive three
dollars a week and board and lessons, the neighbors
became interested and encouraged him to go ahead,
they promising to help look after the farm and see that
the family got along. The young man's happiness
over these events can better be imagined than described.

On the second day of October, 1838, he entered upon
his duties in his new heaven on earth located at Harmony Hall, Mr. Johnson's music-room, in Boston. His
duties were to see to the fires, care for the room, answer callers, give information about Mr. Johnson when
he was out, and practice his lessons when not otherwise
engaged. He worked industriously and made steady
progress. It was but a few weeks till Mr. Johnson had
him playing for the prayer-meeting, and but a few
more till he began turning over pupils to him. In
about seven weeks' time Mr. Johnson encouraged him
by a considerable increase of salary. A most important event to him was meeting Dr. Lowell Mason and
being accepted as a bass singer in the celebrated Bowdoin Street choir. Also, on Mr. Johnson's recommendation, he began taking private voice lessons of
Mr. Geo. Jas. Webb, the then celebrated voice teacher
of Boston. He continued at least a year with Mr. Webb.

His first real singing class was taught the following
fall, 1839, at the North End. It lasted nearly through
the winter, and on the closing night his class made him
a present of a silver goblet, suitably engraved, which
he kept among his treasures.

Before the first year was up Mr. Johnson proposed a
five year partnership, by which Mr. Root was to receive
one-third of their earnings, and the former was to have

the privilege of visiting Germany part of the time if
he chose.   They then changed their quarters to three
rooms in the basement of Park Street Church.   The
annual rental was six hundred dollars.   They were kept
quite busy.

At this time Dr. Mason's music teaching in the
public schools was a growing success, and Messrs.
Johnson and Root were employed to assist him.   Drs.
Mason and Webb had introduced what is now called
Musical Conventions a year or two previous to this.
They called them "The Teachers' Class."   Teachers
and singers were called to Boston from surrounding
territory to study and practice pretty much as they do
now at normals.

In 1841 Mr. Root became one of the teachers in this
class.   He taught vocal training and continued this
work for years afterwards in Dr. Mason's teachers'
classes, and later incorporated the same method in his
own normals.   During this year Mr. Johnson went to
Germany, and left the two large church choirs (Winter
Street and Park Street) in charge of Mr. Root.   One of
the organs was played by a pupil—Mr. S. A. Bancroft.

Everything went smoothly during Mr. Johnson's ab-
sence as it did also after his return.   During the last
year of the five-year partnership, Mr. Root was called
to take the organ at Bowdoin Street, Mr. Mason
changing to Winter Street.   An amicable settlement
was made between Messrs. Johnson and Root, and the
partnership dissolved.

In 1844, Mr. Jacob Abbott (father of Lyman Abbott)
and his three brothers had established a young ladies'
school in New York City.   They wanted a music teacher,
and offered the position to Mr. Root.   They also se-

cured him the organ and choir of the Mercer Street Church, with prospects for other good work. It required pretty strong persuasive arguments to tempt Mr. Root to leave Boston. He was doing well there, and as the sequel shows, there was an attraction in Boston that held him in too tight a grasp to be relinquished by the mere offer of greater power and place. He made up his mind, however, only after getting the consent of the powers of Boston to take with him this [to him] the greatest attraction of the city—Miss Mary Olive Woodman—an accomplished lady, a sweet singer, and a member of a prominent family of musicians. He went to New York first to prepare a home, and in August, 1845, returned for his bride, who took her place in his New York choir as leading soprano, and through his long and eventful career she was ever at his side, a true helpmeet.

He was soon employed at Rutger's Female Institute, Miss Haines' School for Young Ladies, Union Theological Seminary and the New York State Institution for the Blind. Within six weeks after he arrived in New York his time was fully occupied. He continued with Mr. Abbott's young ladies' school ten years.

While teaching in New York he continued his summer work with Messrs. Mason and Webb in Teachers' Classes. Up to the year 1849 he had written but little music ; only a few hymn tunes while in Boston. He needed more music for the young ladies of his schools, so he made his first book, "The Young Ladies' Choir," of which he had enough copies made for his own use, as he had no thought of offering it to the public. Then in connection with Mr. J. E. Sweetser, they compiled the " Root and Sweetser's Collection."

Mr. Root did work enough for two men, hence broke down in health. Mr. Abbott suggested that he take a trip to Paris. After weighing the matter carefully, in December, 1853, he sailed, and in due time arrived at Paris, where he began studying French, voice culture and piano under celebrated teachers. After spending nearly a year abroad, he returned home in improved health and ready for active work. He began to feel the need of new music for his classes, and after some thought decided upon a musical play ; the subject and title, " The Flower Queen."

At the Institution for the Blind was a young lady, a former pupil, but now a teacher who had shown some poetical talent. He asked her to help him with the words. He would suggest in prose what the flowers might say and she would put it into rhyme. She did it so well that it seldom needed any alteration. This lady was the now famous Fanny Crosby. The cantata became very popular. About this time Mr. Root wrote a half dozen simple songs for the people. They all sold pretty well, but " Hazel Dell " and " Rosalie, the Prairie Flower," became the most popular, and had a large sale.

It was in the summer of 1853 that the first real normal was held. Mr. Root originated it, and held it in New York. The principal teachers were Messrs. Mason, Root, Hastings, and Bradbury. This school became famous. Sessions were also held at North Reading, Mass., a village near Mr. Root's " Willow Farm Home," with Dr. Mason, Mr. Webb, Mr. Bradbury and himself as principal teachers.

About this time Mr. Root decided to give up his work in New York, and devote himself entirely to conventions, normal work and authorship. He was eminently successful. Among the most eminent teachers and composers of our country have been students in Dr. Geo. F. Root's Normal Musical Institute.

In 1860 Dr. Root settled in Chicago and entered the music publishing business with his brother E. T. Root, and C. M. Cady, as " Root & Cady," Mr. Root's reputation being the most important capital of the firm. His books and popular songs soon made the new firm prosperous. Then came the war with its horror. Dr. Root wielded his musical sword in the way of writing war songs, which made him famous. " The Battle Cry of Freedom," " Just Before the Battle, Mother," and others, made thousands of dollars for the music house.

In the great Chicago fire of 1871 the interests of the firm of Root & Cady became engulfed in the general ruin. Their loss was upward of a quarter of a million dollars. They then sold their book catalogue, plates and copyrights to John Church & Co., of Cincinnati, and the sheet music plates and copyrights to S. Brainard's Sons, Cleveland. These sales realized about $130,-000. The final result was that Dr. Root, his talented son F. W., and others became connected with John Church & Co. Under this new business relationship Mr. Root went right on with his normal and convention work ; also issued a great many new books and cantatas. In 1872 the Chicago University very worthily conferred upon him the degree Doctor of Music.

In 1886 he made a trip to Scotland and England, and arranged with publishers to issue some of his cantatas. He was royally received.

Dr. Root was the author of about seventy-five books, nearly two hundred songs in sheet form, and many popular gospel songs. Dr. Root occupies a prominent place in the musical history of this country.   It was Dr. Mason who lifted music from almost nothing and gave it an impetus, but he left no better follower than Dr. Root to carry on his work.   He was a man of spotless integrity and high Christian character; and to know him was to love him.

At the time of Dr. Root's death he was at Bailey Island, Maine, a summer resort, where he and other relatives had cottages.   On August 6, 1895, he was seized with neuralgia of the heart—and died within one hour.   He was buried at North Reading, Mass., his old home.

" Dead he is not, but departed—for the artist never dies."

FANNY J. CROSBY.

IV

Miss Fanny J. Crosby

ONE of the great powers that influence the world is the writer of favorite songs and hymns. Such a person approaches nearer to the hearts of the people than any one else. Wherever the religion of Christ has found lodgment the countless songs of Fanny Crosby, the subject of this sketch, have brought comfort to Christian hearts and stirred up inspiration that will abide as long as life shall last.

Frances Jane Crosby, the daughter of John and Mercy Crosby, was born in Southeast, Putnam County, N. Y., March 24, 1820. She became blind at the age of six weeks from maltreatment of her eyes during a spell of sickness. When she was eight years old she moved with her parents to Ridgefield, Conn., the family remaining there four years. At the age of fifteen she entered the New York Institution for the Blind, where she received a good education. She became a teacher in the institution in 1847, and continued her work until March 1, 1858. She taught English grammar, rhetoric, Roman and American history. This was the great developing period in her life. During the vacations of 1852 and 1853, spent at North Reading, Mass., she wrote the words to many songs for Dr. Geo. F. Root, then the teacher of music at the blind institution. Among them were, "Hazel Dell," "The Honeysuckle Glen," "Rosalie, the Prairie Flower," "Music in the Air," "Proud

World, Good-bye, I'm Going Home," "All Together," "Never Forget the Dear Ones," and others. Subsequently she wrote the words for the cantatas of "The Flower Queen" and "The Pilgrim Fathers," all of which were very popular in their day, though it was not generally known at the time that she was the author.

While teaching at the institution she met Presidents Van Buren and Tyler, Hon. Henry Clay, Governor Wm. H. Seward, General Winfield Scott, and other distinguished characters of American history. Concerning Mr. Clay, she gives the following: "When Mr. Clay came to the institution during his last visit to New York, I was selected to welcome him with a poem. Six months before he had lost a son at the battle of Monterey, and I had sent him some verses. In my address I carefully avoided any allusion to them, in order not to wound him. When I had finished he drew my arm in his, and, addressing the audience, said through his tears: 'This is not the first poem for which I am indebted to this lady. Six months ago she sent me some lines on the death of my dear son.' Both of us were overcome for a few moments. Soon, by a splendid effort, Mr. Clay recovered himself, but I could not control my tears." In connection with her meeting these notable men, we might add that Miss Fanny Crosby had the honor of being the first woman whose voice was heard publicly in the Senate Chamber at Washington. She read a poem there on one occasion. In addition to the thousands of hymns that she has written (about eight thousand poems in all), many of which have not been set to music, she has published four volumes of verses. The first was issued in 1844,

and was entitled " The Blind Girl, and Other Poems " ;
a second volume, " Monterey, and Other Poems," followed in 1849, and the third, " A Wreath of Columbia's Flowers," in 1858. The fourth, " Bells at Evening
and Other Verses," with a biographical sketch by Rev.
Robert Lowry, and a fine half-tone portrait, in 1897,
the sales of which have reached a fourth edition. The
book is published by The Biglow & Main Co., New
York.

Though these show the poetical bent of her mind,
they have little to do with her world-wide fame. It is
as a writer of Sunday-school songs and gospel hymns
that she is known wherever the English language is
spoken, and, in fact, wherever any other language is
heard.

Fanny was married March 5, 1858, to Alex. Van
Alstyne, who was also a scholar in the same institution
in which she was educated.

She began to write Sunday-school hymns for Wm. B.
Bradbury in 1864. Her first hymn,

> " We are going, we are going
> To a home beyond the skies,"

was written at the Ponton Hotel on Franklin Street, New
York City, on February 5th of that year. This hymn
was sung at Mr. Bradbury's funeral in January, 1868.

Since 1864 she has supported herself by writing
hymns. She has resided in New York City nearly all
her life, where, she says, she is " a member of the Old
John Street M. E. Church in good standing." She
spends regular hours on certain days at the office of
The Biglow & Main Co., the firm for which she does
most of her writing, and for whom she has composed

over four thousand hymns. Her hymns have been in great demand and have been used by many of our most popular composers, among whom may be mentioned Wm. B. Bradbury, Geo. F. Root, W. H. Doane, Rev. Robert Lowry, Ira D. Sankey, J. R. Sweney, W. J. Kirkpatrick, H. P. Main, H. P. Danks, Philip Phillips, B. C. Unseld, and others. She can compose at any time and does not need to wait for any special inspiration, and her best hymns have come on the spur of the moment. She always composes with an open book in her hand, generally a copy of "Golden Hymns," held closely over her eyes, bottom side up. She learned to play on the guitar and piano while at the institution, and has a clear soprano voice. She also received a technical training in music, and for this reason she can, and does, compose airs for some of her hymns. One of these is,

> " Jesus, dear, I come to Thee,
>   Thou hast said I may,"

both words and music of which are wonderfully sweet. "Safe in the arms of Jesus," probably one of her best known hymns, is her own favorite.

Fanny loves her work, and is happy in it. She is always ready either to sympathize or join in a mirthful conversation, as the case may be. The secret of this contentment dates from her first composition at the age of eight years. "It has been the motto of my life," she says. It is:

> " O what a happy soul am I !
>   Although I cannot see,
>   I am resolved that in this world
>   Contented I will be ;

> How many blessings I enjoy
>   That other people *don't!*
> To weep and sigh because I'm blind,
>   I cannot, and I won't."

This has continued to be her philosophy. She says that had it not been for her affliction she might not have so good an education, nor so great an influence, and certainly not so fine a memory. She knows a great many portions of the Bible by heart, and had committed to memory the first four books of the Old Testament, and also the four Gospels before she was ten years of age.

Her scope of subjects is wide, embracing everything from a contemplation of heaven, as in "The Bright Forever" and "The Blessed Homeland," to an appeal to the work of this world, as in "To the Work" and "Rescue the Perishing." The most of Fanny's published hymns have appeared under the name of Fanny J. Crosby or Mrs. Van Alstyne, but quite a large number have appeared under the *nom de plumes* of Grace J. Frances, Mrs. C. M. Wilson, Lizzie Edwards, Ella Dale, Henrietta E. Blair, Rose Atherton, Maud Marion, Leah Carlton, nearly two hundred different names.

Among her most widely-known hymns may be named the following : "There's a cry from Macedonia," "I feel like singing all the time," "Never be afraid to speak for Jesus," "Lord, at Thy mercy seat," "Jesus the water of life will give," "'Give,' said the little stream," "We are marching on with shield and banner bright," "Pass me not, O gentle Saviour," "Jesus, keep me near the cross," "Rescue the Perishing," "Sing with a tuneful spirit," "Praise Him, praise Him," "To the work, to the work," "The Bright Forever," "Blessed Assurance," "Close to Thee," "Blessed Homeland," "Saved by Grace," "Thy word is a lamp to my feet, O Lord," "Hast thou trimmed thy lamp, my brother?" "Never say good-bye."

Mr. Van Alstyne (her husband) was said to be a good musician. He died in 1902. Fanny is extremely young for her age, and she laughingly avers that she "will live to be 103." When her time comes to pass into the glory-world, her eyes will be opened, and she "shall see Him face to face, and tell the story—Saved by grace."

DR. L. O. EMERSON.

V

Dr. L. O. Emerson

LUTHER ORLANDO EMERSON was born at
Parsonsfield, Maine, August 3, 1820. He de-
scended from distinguished English ancestry.
His parents were quite musical, and while the family
circle were together, they had a choir and orchestra of
their own. The father played the violincello, the
mother was an excellent singer, the flute and violin
added their sweet tones, till the quiet homestead rang
with melody.

Mr. Emerson's education was obtained at the district
school, Parsonsfield Seminary and Effingham Academy.
He was full of energy, quick and versatile, an apt
scholar, and with a view to entering the profession of
medicine he entered Dracut Academy, Mass. But his
great love for music swerved him from that course, and
now, having far better opportunities for cultivating
and enjoying this taste and ability, he soon determined
upon music as the profession of his choice. He accordingly commenced a course of musical instruction under
the late I. B. Woodbury, then a popular teacher of
music. After several years of study on the voice, piano,
organ and in harmony, Mr. Emerson went to Salem,
Mass., began teaching, and took charge of his first choir
at a salary of one hundred dollars per year. Here he
commenced the composition of music for his own choir,
which was so popular with its members and the con-

gregation, that Mr. Emerson was encouraged to seek a
larger hearing by publishing a collection of church
music. Among the tunes was that of "Sessions,"
named after his pastor, which was destined to have a
perennial popularity, and is often used in worship in
the place of "Old Hundred," for the Doxology. At
the great Peace Jubilee it was received with applause
when sung by a chorus of ten thousand voices, accompanied by an orchestra of two hundred instruments and
a great pipe organ. The effect was sublime beyond
expression.

In 1847 occurred the marriage of Mr. Emerson to
Miss Mary Gore, daughter of a prominent Boston mer-
chant. She was a lady of much musical taste and
ability.

In 1853 he decided to make an effort to put his music
before the public, and accordingly went to Boston in
search of a publisher. Like most young and unknown
authors, he met with but little encouragement; but
finally found a publisher in the person of Mr. B. B.
Muzzy. Thus was the "Romberg Collection" published.
The book was not pushed—hence it found no market.

After a residence of eight years in Salem, Mr. Emerson removed to Boston, accepting the position of
organist and musical director at the Bulfinch Street
Church, then under the pastoral care of Rev. Wm. R.
Alger, which he filled for four years. He eagerly improved the rare means of culture which were once
more enjoyed, meanwhile teaching and composing
music.

In 1857 he formed the connection with Oliver Ditson
Company, of Boston, of author and publisher, which has
continued to the present time with but one interruption

(a single volume brought out by another firm), the
" Golden Wreath," which at once became popular, and
sold forty thousand during the first year, this being the
initial volume in the long series since brought out by
these publishers. In 1858 came the " Golden Harp,"
which was also a success. These successes gave him not
only encouragement, but reputation.

Mr. Emerson now entered upon a career of usefulness
and popularity for which he had been preparing during
the years of self-denying struggle and discipline. He
was called to take charge of the music in the Second
Congregational Church, Greenfield, Mass., and also of
the musical department of Power's Institute, at
Bernardston. Amid nature's most beautiful surroundings, he had a quiet retreat for the pursuit of his true
vocation, the composition of church music.

The first fruit of his genius here was the " Sabbath
Harmony," in 1860. This book was also a success. In
1863 followed the " Harp of Judah," which had the remarkable sale of nearly fifty thousand copies in the first
three months. This book probably gave Mr. Emerson
his preëminence as a composer of church music, containing as it did his anthem, " Guide Me, O Thou
Great Jehovah," and many of his finest compositions.

Having declined the solicitations of Dr. Lowell
Mason to become his associate in music, Mr. Emerson
started forth on his own plans, and attained the highest rank among those who loved the pure and beautiful in song. Mr. W. S. B. Mathews, a musical critic,
pronounces him the best melodist of all the psalmody
writers.

In 1866 the equally successful " Jubilate " appeared, followed by the " Choral Tribute," the " Stand-

ard " and the " Leader." In the last two Dr. H. R. Palmer was associated with him. Later on came the " Salutation," " Voice of Worship," " Herald of Praise," etc. The diligence with which Mr. Emerson plied his pen can be estimated when one recalls the fact that he has made seventy-two collections of music, embracing music for churches, singing schools, public schools, choral societies and conventions, instruction books for voice, organ, etc. He has also composed and published scores of songs, quartets and instrumental pieces.

The great amount of work this represents can only be appreciated by those who have undertaken similar labors. Some years ago the degree of Doctor of Music was conferred upon Professor Emerson by the Faculty of Findlay College, Findlay, Ohio.

For many years past, Dr. Emerson has devoted his energies to the grand purpose of elevating the general character of music in our churches, and thus largely advancing the interests of true worship. He places great stress upon the mission of church music. He regards sacred music as the best expression of devotional feeling that exists. He looks upon sacred song as prayer, and believes that it inspires and intensifies prayer. With this view he has taken an active and prominent part in musical festivals and conventions, of which he has conducted over three hundred throughout the United States and Canada. As a conductor, he stands in the front rank. As a teacher, Dr. Emerson has an exceedingly happy faculty of imparting in a concise manner to his classes. His very pleasing address enables him to command the undivided attention of his pupils.

As a singer, he has always held high rank, and has

sung much in public.   His voice is a baritone of great
compass, and quite powerful.   As a lecturer upon
music, Dr. Emerson has attracted much attention.   His
most popular lecture is entitled : " The World of
Music," in which he traces its origin and progress, and
gives some excellent traits of the lives of the great composers.   In this lecture he also shows the design of
music, and how it has been prized in every age of the
world, among all nations—its power in the Church and
State, and the need of its influence in the family—in
joy and sorrow—for this life and the life to come.

Dr. Emerson resides in Hyde Park, a suburb of Boston, where he has a most pleasant home, and enjoys a
large circle of friends and an honored reputation.
Though full of years, he is also full of life and vigor,
and labors with unabated zeal in editing books and
composing music.

Dr. Emerson's two daughters are very fine musicians.   They are composers, directors of music clubs,
and have issued several music books for children.

Dr. Emerson is a great and good man, and has used
his gifts in promoting the Master's cause in sacred song.

REV. W. O. CUSHING.

VI

Rev. W. O. Cushing

THE subject of this sketch, William Orcutt Cushing, was born at Hingham Center, Mass., December 31, 1823. His parents were Unitarians, and his early training was along these lines, having studied with the Unitarian minister at his home town. William was a most noble and thoughtful boy, and when he became old enough to read the Bible and think for himself, he joined the Christian Church.

When eighteen years of age he decided to prepare for the ministry, feeling that he had a call from God to that work. After completing his education he entered upon the work for his Master. Mr. Cushing's first pastorate was at Searsburg, N. Y. While here he became acquainted with Miss Hena Proper, and was married to her February 4, 1854. She proved to be a great help to him in his gospel work. After serving Searsburg charge for several years, he was at different times pastor at Auburn, Brooklyn, Buffalo, and Sparta, N. Y. During these years of faithful work, Mrs. Cushing's health failed; they then returned to Searsburg, where he again served as pastor for several years. After a long illness through which he cared tenderly for her, she died July 13, 1870. Soon after her death, creeping paralysis seized upon Mr. Cushing, and he was compelled to retire from the ministry.

As a pastor, he was very successful, and dearly beloved by both old and young; he was also a great worker in the Sunday-school. After being incapacitated for active ministerial work, his prayer was, "Lord, still give me something to do for Thee!" In answer to this prayer he was permitted to write many of the world's best known gospel poems. Rev. W. O. Cushing wrote over three hundred hymns that have been set to music by some of the most distinguished composers of this country, including Dr. Geo. F. Root, Rev. Robert Lowry, Ira D. Sankey, H. P. Main and others. Perhaps the most widely known of his hymns are the following: "Ring the Bells of Heaven," "We are Waiting, We are Watching," "When He Cometh," "Hiding in Thee," "Do They Know?" "There'll be no Dark Valley," "When Jesus Comes," "Down in the Valley," "Beautiful Valley of Eden," "I am Waiting by the River," "The Name of Jesus," "Fair is the Morning Land," "Gathering Home to the Silent Shore," Children's Day service—"Floral Praise." His hymns have added a rich contribution to American hymnology, and are sung wherever the gospel in song may be found.

Mr. Cushing was a most noble, sweet spirited Christian gentleman. To know him was to love him. He was ever mindful of the suffering of others, but was oblivious to his own. It was a characteristic of his life to minister to the wants of others, and trust the Lord to supply his own. At one time he gave a thousand dollars, which was all he had, to a blind girl that she might secure an education. He was instrumental in the erection of the Seminary at Starkey, N. Y., and also gave material aid to the school for the blind at Batavia.

Mr. Cushing was poor in purse, but rich in spirit; homeless, but not friendless. The last thirteen years of his life were spent in the home of Rev. and Mrs. E. E. Curtis, Lisbon Center, N. Y. While living with these good people, he united with the Wesleyan Methodist Church. He died October 19, 1902. His life was an inspiration to all who knew him, and his death was that of the righteous.

MRS. HARRIET E. JONES.

VII

Mrs. Harriet E. Jones

THE name of Harriet E. Jones is known and honored by the great army of Christian workers in all lands. Wherever the gospel song has gone her name and influence have been felt. And what an honor it is to have written hymns that have cheered the hearts of saints and called sinners to repentance the world over, thus being a " worker together with God " and His chosen people in extending His kingdom in the world!

Mrs. Jones deserves all the love and esteem her good work has brought her. She is such a true Christian, with such a sunshiny disposition that to know her or to be associated with her in any way is to be benefited. She has passed through sore afflictions and trials, but these have served to reveal to her the goodness of God, and to draw her closer to Him. Her trials have really sweetened her character.

She was the daughter of Eleazer Rice, and was born April 18, 1823. She has always lived in Onondaga County, N. Y. Her post-office is Oran. Her girlhood was spent on a farm, receiving what education the country schools and one term at high school afforded. She was always fond of reading, and read a great deal. From early childhood she was a great singer, being passionately fond of music and possessed with a clear, ringing voice, and would have distinguished herself as a soloist if she would have had the advantages of vocal training. For years she sang regularly in the home choir.

On July 7, 1844, she was married to a son of Rev. Zenus Jones. Mrs. Jones' husband died in 1879. While passing through the waters of affliction and sorrow she wrote some verses. They were published, and attracted the attention of Dr. M. J. Munger, of Rochester, N. Y., who was at that time compiling a book of Sunday-school songs with A. J. Abbey. He wrote Mrs. Jones, complimenting her on her poetry, and asked her to write some Sunday-school hymns for him. She consented, and by his help in suggesting topics and by kindly criticisms and hints she made a success of it.

She next wrote for Mr. D. B. Towner, J. C. Ewing and Fillmore Brothers, and from that she received calls from almost all the composers and publishers, so that now her hymns are found in all the best gospel and Sunday-school song books.

Mrs. Jones is an enthusiastic Methodist and Prohibitionist. For many years she has been closely confined to her home by the care of an invalid son, but she never complains, but writes hymns, and sings the tunes that various composers set to them, and rejoices at the kind words that come to her from many sources testifying to the great happiness others receive from her inspirations.

Among the many popular hymns she has written we mention "Redeemed." These words express her experience when she was converted. They abound in exclamations of joy and rapture, just the kind to inspire the most. popular music. Mr. D. B. Towner caught its inspiration for music, and it has been one of his leading songs for many years past. At the great

Moody meetings it was very popular and a general favorite. Other singing evangelists have used it with great power. Some others are: " Blue Sea of Galilee," music by Davis; "The Song of Love," music by Meredith; " Harbor Home" and " At the Pool of Siloam," music by Entwisle; "There is Sweet Rest " and " Trusting in the Blessed Christ," music by Hall.

We don't believe we can close this brief sketch better than by quoting a paragraph from one of her letters :

" I am trying in my imperfect way to serve the Master, and hope to live with Him by and by, and be able to enjoy the sweet music for which I have vainly longed through the toilsome, lonely years.

> " ' Some souls go hungering through the years,
>   And never find the food they seek.'

But over beyond in the home of our God is sweet fruition. There is the music of angels, fadeless flowers, green fields, and still waters and, what is better, reunion with loved ones, sweetest of all, the presence of the King and the glad redemption song, in which I hope to join."

T. C. O'KANE.

VIII

T. C. O'Kane

AMONG all the popular gospel and Sunday-school song writers of our times, no one is more widely known or holds a higher place in the affections of the Christian world than T. C. O'Kane. He was one among the very first to strike out with more freedom in his melodies and rhythms, and introduce the style of songs that have since taken such a strong hold upon the people, and that have been the great moving power in religious revivals and great religious convocations.

Tullius Clinton O'Kane was born in Fairfield County, Ohio, March 10, 1830. He resided with his parents in this vicinity until the spring of 1849, when he went to Delaware, Ohio, and entered the Ohio Wesleyan University, from which he graduated in 1852, with the degree A. B., and received his A. M. degree three years later from his Alma Mater.

Immediately upon his graduation, he was tendered a position in the Faculty as Tutor of Mathematics, which he accepted and successfully filled for five years. The students always called him "Professor," by which title he is known to the present day.

His musical abilities were early recognized in the University, and for years he was the musical precentor in the daily chapel devotions. He organized and maintained a Choral Society in the College, and was the first musical instructor in the Ohio Wesleyan Female College, which a few years ago was incorporated into the University.

In 1857 he was elected to a principalship in the Cincinnati public schools, and served in that capacity until 1864, when he resigned his position to accept a place in the piano establishment of Philip Phillips & Co. He remained with this house until its removal to New York City in 1867, when, although urged to be transferred with the house to that city, he preferred to remove with his family back to Delaware, Ohio, where he now resides.

For the ensuing six years he travelled over the state of Ohio as the general agent for the Smith American Organ Co., of Boston, Mass. During this time he visited conferences, Sunday-school conventions, both State and County, introducing his Sunday-school singing books, and in this way became well known throughout his native state, and quite extensively in some of the adjoining states.

His musical compositions were first published in Philip Phillips' "Musical Leaves," in 1865, and since then but few Sunday-school singing books have appeared without one or more of his compositions.

His first music book, "Fresh Leaves," was issued in 1868. This was followed at intervals by "Dew Drops," "Songs of Worship," "Every Sabbath," "Jasper and Gold," "Redeemer's Praise," "Glorious Things" and "Morning Stars." In connection with his son, Edward T. O'Kane, who is himself a most excellent composer and a very skillful organist, in 1882 he issued "Selected Anthems," a book designed for use by the more advanced choirs. In association with J. R. Sweney and "Chaplain" McCabe, he issued "Joy to the World," a song book for prayer-meetings, and the same editors, with the addition of W. J. Kirkpatrick, compiled "Songs of Redeeming Love, No. 1," in 1882, and No. 2 in 1887. He also issued " Songs of Praises," " Unfading Treasures " and " Forward Songs."

Some of Professor O'Kane's best known songs are: " Glorious Fountain," " The Home Over There," " On Jordan's Stormy Banks," " Say, are You Ready ?" and many others. With Mr. O'Kane, music and musical composition have ever been a recreation, rather than a profession. He is an excellent leader of choirs, but his forte seems to be in leading large congregations, Sunday-schools and social religious meetings in sacred song. He sings " with the spirit and the understanding also "—with a due appreciation of both words and music—and very naturally infuses his enthusiasm into his audiences so that they cannot " keep from singing." In his music he endeavors to catch the spirit of the hymn, and then give it expression in the music he composes for it. This sometimes seems to have been almost an inspiration, and could be illustrated by a reference to the circumstances under which many of his compositions have been made.

One of his earlier and more widely known pieces is that entitled, " Over There." He says he cut this hymn out of some newspaper and put it with others in his portfolio, intending some time when he felt like it to give it a musical setting. One Sunday afternoon, after studying his lesson for the next session of his Sunday-school, he opened his portfolio, and turning over the selections, found these words, and something seemed to say, "Now's your time." He sat down at the organ, studied the hymn intently for a few moments, and then, as his fingers touched the keys of the instrument, melody and harmony were in every movement, and when the stanza was ended, melody and harmony found their expression in the chorus, and "Over There" was finished.

Another of his well known songs is "Sweeping Through the Gates." One cold, blustery day he had occasion to go from his residence to the railroad depot, about a mile distant, and in his route had to cross the river on a suspension foot-bridge. As he came down to the bridge, he thought of the "river of death," so cold, with no bridge, and then the words of the dying Cookman came to his mind, and he exclaimed to himself:

"Who, who are these beside the chilly wave?"

Words, melody and refrain seemed to come all at once and all together, so that by the time he arrived back at his home, the composition was complete.

Professor O'Kane is a genial, modest, Christian gentleman, who carries sunshine wherever he goes. His greatest joy comes from the consciousness that his music has cheered and comforted the hearts of Christian people all over the world, and has been the means of winning thousands from the pleasures of the world to the higher enjoyments of the Christian religion. His song, "Sweeping Through the Gates," will be sung till all the ransomed are gathered "Over There."

NOTE.—Soon after we had finished the above sketch Prof. T. C. O'Kane passed away quite suddenly at the home of his son, Mr. E. T. O'Kane.

On the morning of February 10, 1912, immediately after family devotions, in which Professor O'Kane led and closing with the Lord's Prayer, he started for his room when heart failure seized him and he fell unconscious and in a few minutes his spirit had taken its flight to his "Home Over There." How beautiful and peculiarly appropriate that he went home with the "Amen" of his Master's great prayer as his last spoken word.

T. E. PERKINS.

IX

Theodore E. Perkins

THE subject of this sketch was born at Pough-keepsie, on the Hudson, N. Y., July 21, 1831. His father was a Baptist clergyman. The family of ten brothers and sisters sang and played various instruments, forming among themselves both choir and orchestra. His musical education began at the early age of three years. During his father's pastorate at Hamilton, N. Y., the choir rehearsals were often held at the parsonage, and the leader used to place the three-year-old on a small stool, on the table around which the choir was assembled, giving him a chance to both see and hear. Later on he played the violincello in church, standing on a stool in order to finger the instrument.

The home gatherings—especially on Thanksgiving Day, are the recollections among the happiest of his childhood. His father became pastor of the Berean Baptist Church in New York City, in 1839, giving him the opportunity of studying the pianoforte, of which he became a proficient player. His fine alto voice soon gave him notoriety. At the age of nineteen while filling a position as clerk in New York, all his spare time was given to the study of voice and piano. In 1851 he went to Hamilton, N. Y., taught music in Madison University (now Colgate), and in the Female Seminary.

In 1854 he went to Port Jervis, N. Y., where he taught
singing school, and April 30, 1855, married Mary Frances Caskey, who was for years his soprano soloist in
many musical Festivals and Conventions. Soon after
marriage he removed to Salem, N. J., where his life-
work as singing school teacher really began, including
Bridgeton and prominent towns in southern New
Jersey. During the summer of 1856 he and his wife
were pupils of the Normal Academy of Music at North
Reading, Mass., conducted by Drs. Lowell Mason and
Geo. F. Root. During 1857–1858 he was given the
position of assistant teacher and manager. His association with these two great men gave an inspiration to
all his future work.

In 1859 he was co-principal with Wm. B. Bradbury
at the Normal Academy of Music, Geneseo, N. Y. He
remained at Geneseo until 1863. Professor Perkins
also held very successful schools in North Pelham
Province of Ontario, Canada, and in 1864–1868 was
principal in schools at Tunkhannock and Meadville, Pa.

In 1860, " The Olive Branch," his first book of
church music, was published by F. J. Huntington, New
York City, the sales reaching 100,000. Next was
"Oriental," which sold over 30,000. " The Union,"
" Glees and Anthems," and " Sabbath Anthems," fol-
lowed ; then " The Sacred Lute," which sold over 300,-
000. His Sunday-school books commenced with " The
Evergreen," followed by the " Shining Star " and
" New Shining Star." Then came " Psalm King,"
which was the last of the books published by Mr.
Huntington. " Hallowed Songs " was published by
Philip Phillips ; " The Sunday School Banner " was
published by Wm. B. Bradbury. " The Royal Stand-

ard " was published in Toronto, Canada. " The Golden
Promise," " Sabbath Carols," " The Mount Zion Col-
lection " were published under his own supervision.
His " Free Sunday School Songs " several times
numbered over 500,000 a month. " Coronation Songs "
with Rev. Dr. Deems as hymn editor was published by
A. S. Barnes & Co., who also published " Psalms and
Hymns and Spiritual Songs," in which Dr. C. S. Robin-
son was hymn editor, who with Professor Perkins
edited " Calvary Songs," published by the American
S. S. Union. " Gospel Tent Songs " was evangelical.
" The Safe-Guard Singer " was his temperance book.

Mr. Perkins was musical director in the following
churches in Brooklyn : The Lafayette Avenue Presbyterian Church, Rev. Dr. Cuyler ; Strong Place Baptist
Church, Rev. E. E. L. Taylor, D. D. ; Madison Avenue
Baptist Church, Rev. H. G. Weston, D. D., L. L. D. ;
Fifth Avenue Presbyterian Church, Rev. Dr. Rice, followed by Dr. John Hall ; The Memorial Presbyterian
Church, Rev. Dr. C. S. Robinson, who was his close
friend ; The Church of the Holy Trinity, Rev. Dr.
Tyng, Jr. ; Trinity Baptist Church, Rev. Dr. J. B. Sim-
mons, and Washington Square M. E. Church.

In Philadelphia : The Fifth Baptist Church, Rev. Dr.
Chase ; The Eleventh Baptist Church, Rev. Dr. Col-
man ; The Tabernacle M. E. Church, Rev. George
Gaul, D. D. He was leader and singer in Evangelistic
Services, at the Rink, The Old Madison Square
Garden and Cooper Union, all of New York City.
The music of the first great meeting of the world's
Evangelical Alliance, held for ten days in New York
City, was under his direction, as was the first National
Sunday School convention, held in Newark, N. J. He

was also conductor at the Golden Anniversary of the
Female Guardian Society, leading a chorus of forty-
two hundred children. In the opening chorus, "Great
is the Lord," by Dr. Calcott, the word "Great" was
given with so much decision and power that the clergy-
men on the platform sprang to their feet and remained
standing until the chorus was finished.

He taught voice culture in Princeton and Lafayette
Universities, The Union Theological Seminary, New
York City; Crozer Seminary, Chester, Pa., and organized the music department of Temple University,
Philadelphia, continuing in charge four years. He had
charge of the children's choir of Howard Mission, New
York City, for twenty-five years, and thinks that some
of the happiest and most restful of the working hours
were spent in teaching the poor children of the fourth
and sixth wards to sing the Gospel. Mr. Sankey said
to Mr. Perkins that "'Jesus of Nazareth' was my
banner song for eight years." "Jesus is Mine" has been
sung at the Christian's death-bed, the grave, and once
as the convict was going to the scaffold.

His "Christmas Carol Sweetly Carol" had a very
large sale in this country, and was republished in England, France, Italy, and Germany.

For a period of forty years he has made the study of
the voice special work. The most thorough investigations of the voice and its possibilities were made with
the assistance of the late John Howard, extending over
a period of twenty-five years, during which he has had
the care of over two thousand voices. He published a
work entitled, "Physiological Voice Culture," edited
by his son, the late T. Edward Perkins, M. D., physician and throat specialist of Philadelphia. Mr. Perkins

at this writing has just completed a method of voice
culture based on the principles of John Howard's
" Physiology of Artistic Singing."

During these years of work he has found time to edit
thirty-four books of church, Sunday-school, day-school,
and glee music, the larger portion having been previously mentioned. Also songs and ballads in sheet
form, and a cantata entitled, " The Excursion," libretto
by Fanny Crosby, with whom there has existed an unbroken friendship for over forty years. Mr. and Mrs.
Perkins celebrated their golden wedding anniversary
April 30, 1905.

Prof. T. E. Perkins will be remembered many years
hence by his sweet, inspiring gospel songs.

REV. ROBERT LOWRY.

X

Rev. Robert Lowry, D. D.

THE name of Rev. Robert Lowry is a familiar one in almost every home where gospel songs are sung. The mention of his name brings up emotions of affection and pleasure in the hearts of thousands of Christian people who have used his hymns.

Robert Lowry was born in Philadelphia, March 12, 1826. His fondness for music was exhibited in his earliest years. As a child he amused himself with the various musical instruments that came into his hands. At the age of seventeen he joined the First Baptist Church of Philadelphia, and soon became an active worker in the Sunday-school as teacher and chorister. At the age of twenty-two he gave himself to the work of the ministry, and entered upon a course of study at the University of Lewisburg, Pa. At the age of twenty-eight he was graduated with the highest honors of his class. In the same year of his graduation, he entered upon the work of the ministry. He served as pastor at West Chester, Pa., 1854–1858; in New York City, 1859–1861; in Brooklyn, 1861–1869; in Lewisburg, Pa., 1869–1875. While pastor at Lewisburg, he was also professor of belles lettres in the University, and received the honorary degree of D. D. in 1875.

He then went to Plainfield, N. J., where he became

pastor of Park Avenue Church.   In each of these fields
his work was crowned with marked success.

Dr. Lowry was a man of rare administrative ability,
a most excellent preacher, a thorough Bible student,
and whether in the pulpit or upon the platform, always
a brilliant and interesting speaker.   He was of a genial
and pleasing disposition, and a high sense of humor
was one of his most striking characteristics.   Very few
men had greater ability in painting pictures from the
imagination.   He could thrill an audience with his
vivid descriptions, inspiring others with the same
thoughts that inspired him.

His melodies are sung in every civilized land, and
many of his hymns have been translated into foreign
tongues.   While preaching the Gospel, in which he
found great joy, was his life-work, music and hymnology were favorite studies, but were always a side
issue, a recreation.

In the year 1880, he took a rest of four years, visiting Europe.   In 1885 he felt that he needed more rest,
and resigned his pastorate at Plainfield, and visited in
the South and West, also spending some time in Mexico.
He returned, much improved in health, and again took
up his work in Plainfield.

On the death of Wm. B. Bradbury, Messrs. Biglow
& Main, successors to Mr. Bradbury in the publishing
business, selected Dr. Lowry for editor of their Sunday-
school book, " Bright Jewels," which was a great success.   Subsequently Dr. W. H. Doane was associated
with him in the issue of the Sunday-school song book,
" Pure Gold," the sales of which exceeded a million
copies.   Then came " Royal Diadem," " Welcome Tidings," " Brightest and Best," " Glad Refrain," " Good

as Gold," " Joyful Lays," " Fountain of Song," " Bright
Array," " Temple Anthems," and numerous other volumes. The good quality of their books did much to
stimulate the cause of sacred song in this country.

When he saw that the obligations of musical editor-
ship were laid upon him, he began the study of music
in earnest, and sought the best musical text-books and
works on the highest forms of musical composition.
He possessed one of the finest musical libraries in the
country. It abounded in works on the philosophy and
science of musical sounds. He also had some musical
works in his possession that were over one hundred and
fifty years old.

One of his labors of love some years ago was an attempt to reduce music to a mathematical basis. On the
established fact that Middle C has two hundred and
fifty-six vibrations per second, he prepared a scale and
went to work on the rule of three. After infinite cal-
culation and repeated experiments, he carried it far
enough to discover that it would not work.

A reporter once asked him what was his method of
composition—" Do you write the words to fit the music,
or the music to fit the words ? " His reply was : " I
have no method. Sometimes the music comes and the
words follow, fitted insensibly to the melody. I watch
my moods, and when anything good strikes me, whether
words or music, and no matter where I am, at home or
on the street, I jot it down. Often the margin of a
newspaper or the back of an envelope serves as a note-
book. My brain is a sort of spinning machine, I think,
for there is music running through it all the time. I
do not pick out my music on the keys of an instrument.
The tunes of nearly all the hymns I have written have

been completed on paper before I tried them on the organ. Frequently the words of the hymn and the music have been written at the same time."

The Doctor frequently said that he regarded " Weep. ing Will Not Save Me " as the best and most evangelistic hymn he ever wrote. The following are some of his most popular and sweetest gospel melodies : " Shall We Gather at the River ? " " One More Day's Work for Jesus," " Where is My Wandering Boy To-night ? " " I Need Thee Every Hour," " The Mistakes of My Life," " How Can I Keep from Singing ? " " All the Way My Saviour Leads Me," " Saviour, Thy Dying Love," " We're Marching to Zion," etc. " Shall We Gather at the River ? " is perhaps, without question, the most widely popular of all his songs. Of this Mr. Lowry said : " It is brass band music, has a march movement, and for that reason has become popular, though for myself I do not think much of it." Yet he tells us how, on several occasions, he had been deeply moved by the singing of that hymn. " Going from Harrisburg to Lewisburg once I got into a car filled with half-drunken lumbermen. Suddenly one of them struck up, ' Shall We Gather at the River ? ' and they sang it over and over again, repeating the chorus in a wild, boisterous way. I did not think so much of the music then as I listened to those singers, but I did think that perhaps the spirit of the hymn, the words so flippantly uttered, might somehow survive and be carried forward into the lives of those careless men, and ultimately lift them upward to the realization of the hope expressed in my hymn." " A different appreciation of it was evinced during the Robert Raikes' Centennial. I was in London, and had gone to meeting in the Old Bailey to see some of the most famous Sunday-school workers in the world.   They were present from Europe, Asia, and America.   I sat in a rear seat alone. After there had been a number of addresses delivered in various languages, I was preparing to leave, when the chairman of the meeting announced that the author of 'Shall We Gather at the River?' was present, and I was requested by name to come forward.   Men applauded and women waved their handkerchiefs as I went to the platform.   It was a tribute to the hymn; but I felt, when it was over, that, after all, I had perhaps done some little good in the world, and I felt more than ever content to die when God called."   On Children's Day in Brooklyn, in 1865, this song was sung by over forty thousand voices.

While Dr. Lowry said, "I would rather preach a gospel sermon to an appreciative, receptive congregation than write a hymn," yet in spite of his preferences, his hymns have gone on and on, translated into many languages, preaching and comforting thousands upon thousands of souls, furnishing them expression for their deepest feelings of praise and gratitude to God for His goodness to the children of men.   What he had thought in his inmost soul has become a part of the emotions of the whole Christian world.   We are all his debtors.

Rev. Robert Lowry, D. D., died at his residence in Plainfield, N. J., November 25, 1899.   Dead, yet he lives and his sermons in gospel song are still heard and are doing good.   Dr. Lowry was a great and good man, and his life, well spent, is highly worthy of a place among the world's greatest gospel song and hymn writers.

DR. W. H. DOANE.

XI

Dr. W. H. Doane

THERE is scarcely a place on earth where civilization has pushed its way that the influence of Dr. Doane has not been felt. To almost every soul in civilized countries, some of his songs are familiar, and as it is the Christian missionary chiefly who extends our civilization, we doubt if any of late years have gone forth to the foreign field without some of Dr. Doane's songs as a part of his equipment.

It is one of the marvellous things of this age that the work of man, if it be meritorious, may have an influence on the whole world. If he invents a valuable tool or machine, its use is not limited to any one country. If he writes a beautiful story or song, it is translated into many languages, and its echoes go from lip to lip "the earth around." Thus it is with the music that Dr. Doane has written; it has been carried to all lands where music is enjoyed, and translated into almost all tongues. While some of the millions who sing his music may not know his name, yet the consciousness on his part that he has added to their happiness, and furnished to their emotions wings on which are borne their praises and petitions to our common Father, should be glory enough for him. Almost any of us would be content to say, "Now lettest Thou Thy servant depart in peace," could we take such a view of the influences of our work.

William Howard Doane was born February 3, 1832, in Preston, Conn. His father was head of the firm of Doane & Treat, cotton manufacturers. At the early age of fourteen years he was the chosen leader of the choir of Woodstock Academy, a Congregational school, where he had been placed by his father. During the last year of his stay there he was converted. His mother being a Baptist, he united with that church at Norwich, Conn. In 1847 he became a clerk in his father's office, and three years later engaged himself with the firm of J. A. Fay & Co., manufacturers of wood-working machinery, whose principal office was then at Norwich, Conn. In 1860 he became the managing partner of the firm, with headquarters in Cincinnati, where he has since resided. At the death of the senior partner, the firm became an incorporated company, of which he was made president. It is one of the most extensive businesses in its line, having connections in many of the principal mercantile centres of the world. With such large business interests in his charge it would seem remarkable that he should have gained such eminence in music. But music was in him and it must find expression. It would not be smothered, hence at every stage of his career we find it asserting itself. He composed his first piece of music in his sixteenth year. In 1852 he was conductor of the Norwich Harmonic Society. In 1862 his first book appeared, entitled, "Sabbath School Gems," followed in 1864 by "Little Sunbeams," and in 1867 came that notable book, "Silver Spray," which perhaps was the most popular Sunday-school book of its day. Then followed, in 1868, "Songs of Devotion," for use in churches, which was very popular. He then became associated with

Rev. Robert Lowry in many musical works, most of which were issued by Messrs. Biglow & Main, New York.

Dr. Doane is justly celebrated on account of his Christmas cantatas. He fairly popularized the Christmas cantata business by the issue of one entitled, "Santa Claus," some years ago. The circulation of books bearing his name has been world-wide, and the copies sold are counted by the millions.

Dr. Doane is of medium height, nervous temperament, and rapid in all of his movements; always cheerful, warm-hearted and generous. Coupled with his educational attainments and ripe business experience he is a lover of home, church, and country that has endeared him to lovers of American institutions wherever he is known.

He has a beautiful residence on Mount Auburn, one of the Cincinnati hills, where he lives in happiness with the wife of his youth (she being the daughter of his father's former partner), and two accomplished daughters.

His study, or music room, is a unique feature of his home. It is as complete in all respects as taste, culture, research, and money can make it. As you enter it, over the door in the transom is wrought in ground glass in musical characters the opening strains of " Home, Sweet Home." On the ceiling inside, at various points, are frescoed bits of celebrated musical compositions beautifully and artistically arranged. Fine pictures, mostly of musical subjects, adorn the walls, with a most extensive collection of antique instruments from Egypt, Mexico, Burmah, Japan, Africa, Russia, Turkey, and Syria, some of which are said to be several hundred years old. And here is a grand pipe organ, run by a water motor, and over the organ, in fresco, four measures of the " Hallelujah Chorus." There are also pianos, a cabinet organ, harp and all modern instruments. The library is exceptionally fine, and one of the largest in the country, containing vellum manuscript dating from the eighth century, facsimiles of the original score of Handel's Messiah, and original manuscript and autographs of nearly all the old masters, including Beethoven, Mendelssohn, Mozart, Handel, Meyerbeer, and also Dr. Lowell Mason, Dr. Thomas Hastings, Wm. B. Bradbury, Dr. Geo. F. Root, P. P. Bliss, Rev. Robert Lowry, and other American composers.

Dr. Doane is an active member of the Mount Auburn Baptist Church, Cincinnati, and for several years has been superintendent of its flourishing Sunday-school, one of the largest in the city. Some time since he and his family spent nearly two years in Europe, visiting the Holy Land, the occasion being the exhibiting of some of his machinery at an European exposition, on which, by the way, he took the highest award. The Mount Auburn Sunday-school gave a " welcoming " service on his return. It was a splendid affair. The schoolroom was tastefully decorated, and on the platform sat a large floral ship named the " Majestic," in honor of the one that had brought the Doctor and his family over the ocean on their return, and when he came in they all—little and big—gave him the Chautauqua salute, and proceeded with a specially prepared service that was unique and beautiful. The demonstrations were universal and hearty, and showed that their superintendent had a warm place in their hearts.

Dr. Doane is a liberal man. Among his benefactions

are "Doane Hall" and Doane Academy of Denison University; and he and the late Mr. John Church, of the John Church Co., donated from the receipts of the "Silver Spray" money to purchase the large pipe organ in the Y. M. C. A. Hall in Cincinnati. The organ is called "Silver Spray." Dr. Doane is an active member of the Y. M. C. A., and one of its active supporters.

He writes his music at home of evenings. Yet he carries his little note-book with him, so as to be prepared to note down, wherever he may be, the inspirations that may come to him. His style of music is peculiarly his own, and shows great versatility of talent.

Dr. Doane has compiled some forty books, and has written about twenty-three hundred songs, ballads, cantatas, etc., also a number of vocal and piano pieces in sheet form. Some of his most popular pieces are: "Safe in the Arms of Jesus," "The Old, Old Story," "Pass Me Not," "A Few More Marchings," "More Love to Thee, O Christ," "Every Day and Hour," "Rescue the Perishing," "Near the Cross," "Draw Me Nearer," "Will He Find Us Watching," and many others.

In 1875 Denison University bestowed upon him the title of Doctor of Music.

While the Doctor is well advanced in years, he is still active and enthusiastic. May he live. long to fill his important place at home, and to contribute of his talent and genius to his larger field—the world.

DR. H. S. PERKINS.

XII

Dr. H. S. Perkins

THE subject of this sketch, Henry Southwick Perkins, was born March 20, 1833, in Stockbridge, Vermont. He inherited his musical talent from his parents, his father being a noted singing teacher and his mother an excellent vocalist. His first musical instruction was received from his father. He attended some of the best literary schools in his youthful days. His regular course of study in music for a profession was commenced in 1857, at which time he entered the Boston Music School, graduating in 1861. His specialties as a student were voice, harmony, theory and composition, yet he gave considerable attention to the piano, violin and other instruments.

Being especially fitted by nature and study for conducting and instructing large bodies of singers, Dr. Perkins devoted considerable of the time for over twenty years to conducting musical festivals and conventions throughout the country from Maine to California—several hundred—and in the teaching of normal music schools, which were held in the states of New York, Ohio, Indiana, Wisconsin, Iowa, Colorado, Kansas and Texas. In 1867-1869 he was Professor of Music in the University of Iowa, and was principal of the Iowa Academy of Music at Iowa City for five consecutive years, also of the Kansas Normal Music School for five consecutive summers. Several years ago he received the honorary degree of Doctor of Music.   As a composer of vocal music for the choir, the Sunday-school, the class, the public school, the choral society, convention and festival, Dr. Perkins has been conspicuous for many years, having edited many books, composed songs, quartets, etc., which have become popular and met with a large sale.

Among Dr. Perkins' most popular choir, class and convention books are the following: " The Church Bell," " The Advance," " The New Century," " Glee and Chorus Book," "Graded Music Reader, Numbers 1, 2 and 3," " Perkins' Class and Choir," " Perkins' Graded Anthems," " Model Class Book," " Festival Choruses," " The Climax," " The Song Indicator," etc.   His works especially designed for the Sunday-school are: " Sabbath School Trumpet," " The River of Life," " The Sunnyside," " The Shining River," " The Glorious Tidings," " Palms of Victory," and " Soul Songs."

Among his many popular gospel songs may be mentioned " Whiter Than Snow," which has been published in many languages and effectively used by all evangelists.   " Waiting, Only Waiting," is another very effective and useful song.

Dr. Perkins was one of the organizers of the Music Teachers' National Association in 1876, read an essay upon " The Object of Musical Association," has served in nearly every official capacity and as secretary for ten years since 1887.   He also organized the Illinois Music Teachers' Association in 1886, was chosen president, and has been reëlected each year for ten consecutive years.   He is regarded as one of the most practical business men in the musical profession.

Dr. Perkins has been a prominent resident of Chicago

since 1872. He has been conspicuous as a musical critic, having been connected with the Chicago press for several years, and a correspondent of papers in other large cities. He travelled extensively in Europe ; studied the methods of instruction pursued in schools and conservatories and delivered many lectures upon his travels and subjects connected with the music teaching profession. In 1891 he established the Chicago National College of Music, in Chicago, in which those who are preparing for teachers, or for artists in any branch of the profession secure a practical course of training. The college has a large and well-equipped faculty and its success has been such as to entitle it to a place among the best in the country.

Socially and musically Dr. Perkins stands among the first in the profession, a man of energy, talent and efficiency. He has accomplished a great work in the " vineyard of song."

DR. H. R. PALMER.

XIII

Dr. H. R. Palmer

D<small>R.</small> HORATIO RICHMOND PALMER, the well-known author and composer, was a man of peculiar and diversified abilities and won distinction in many departments of music. The records show he was born in Sherburne, N. Y., April 26, 1834. By the death of his mother he was left half orphan when little more than two years old. For a time he was tenderly cared for by his mother's sister. Then changes came and during his entire youth he faced the world single handed and alone. He acquired his musical education by hard unremitting study with little assistance. He sang in his father's choir when nine years of age, commenced conducting and composing at eighteen. He married Miss Lucia A. Chapman, a student in Rushford Academy, N. Y., where he was Principal of Music. Mr. Palmer was playing the organ and directing the choir in the Baptist Church at Rushford, N. Y., when a request came from Centerville, a neighboring town, asking him to teach a singing school. He answered the call with fear and trembling, having decided years before that it was not his forte to teach. However, the first lesson went along in a manner satisfactory to all except the teacher.

At the intermission it seemed to Mr. Palmer that everything had gone wrong. He was utterly discour-

aged and was considering stopping then and there, giving it up and running away, when a friend (Mrs. James
Cole) came to where the disheartened young leader was
sitting alone in a most gloomy state of mind.   She was
hearty in praise of the lesson thus far.   " It was delightful, way ahead of anything ever given there before,"
etc., etc.   Taking courage from her enthusiasm he finished the lesson and the term.   At the final concert the
chorus acquitted itself finely, and at once Mr. Palmer
was engaged to return the next year.

Having met with such success he was immediately
besieged with requests to teach singing classes in adjoining localities and states.

For the purpose of enlarging his field of labor he
located for a time in Chicago where he edited a musical
monthly journal, wrote books, and conducted festivals
and associations.   He began this work in 1865 shortly
after the war.   At that time of increasing life and prosperity the desire for music awakened also and demanded
attention, conventions sprang up here and there and
quickly became the social events of city, town and
country districts.   In this work Dr. Palmer was foremost and it grew to gigantic proportions.

He held music schools, normal courses in training
and conducting musical conventions and festivals.   This
work extended over all the Northern states and some
of the Provinces of Canada ; one week he would be in
the West, the next in the East a thousand miles distant
and in the meanwhile his books kept the presses running
continually.   He never missed an engagement for any
of these musical festivals although often required to
make a journey of hundreds of miles, sometimes driving
through snow across country to make trains, when other

connections failed. He never permitted anything to come between him and his aim. He went into everything he undertook with all his heart, loving it, intent upon it, knowing no such word as fail—not recognizing it if it stared him in the face, but walking calmly over it and on to success.

He has carried music and musical enthusiasm to thousands who were otherwise beyond its reach. He has encouraged and helped many hundreds of music students, by instructions, example and personal kindness, to work on against all discouragements, to attain the heights they desired. Scattered all over the country we find leading teachers and conductors who gratefully acknowledge their indebtedness to this loved educator.

The fruitage of this work is what might naturally have been expected from this keen, tactful, energetic, courageous man.

In 1873 he returned to New York City, since which time, accompanied by Mrs. Palmer, he visited Europe three times, once having extended his travels into the Orient. He spent nearly three years in different capitals and musical centres of Europe, studying and investigating the best methods of teaching, listening to operas and concerts given by the best artists, and rendered under the direction of the most able drillmasters in the world.

Dr. Palmer was beyond doubt one of the best-equipped teachers of music in the country. His large and discriminating experience put him in possession of knowledge that cannot be purchased. He was familiar with all the standard operas and oratorios, has adapted and compiled most of the practical excerpts, and unques-

tionably could lay his hand on more fine choruses and
put them to immediate use than most men in the
profession.

In 1881 Dr. Palmer organized the Church Choral
Union in New York City. The aim of the organization was to elevate the class of music used in churches.
Dr. Palmer brought to this work twenty-five years'
experience in handling large gatherings of singers and
the methods which such experience and practical usefulness had developed. No wonder that it grew from
two hundred and fifty the first season to forty-two
hundred the third. Brooklyn, Buffalo, Washington,
Philadelphia and other cities called him and his assist-
ants to start the same kind of work there. The Church
Choral Union was made up from two hundred and
twenty churches, the total number of singers reaching
upwards of twenty thousand, thus forming the largest
church music organization in this country. Dr. Palmer
solved the difficult problem of church music. At one of
his mammoth concerts in Madison Square Garden, during the period in which he had charge of the Church
Choral Union of New York City, he had nearly four
thousand singers on the stage, while the audience filled
the remaining portion of the vast auditorium. It consisted mostly of churchgoing people, and New York
never saw a more refined assemblage.

Dr. Palmer chose the Church for his field of labor
and always had the loyal and liberal support of Christian people. His career was a brilliant one.

Another way in which Dr. Palmer has reached the
homes of thousands of music lovers yearly was through
his Chautauqua work. For fourteen years he had
charge of the music there. He trained and conducted

the marvellous chorus, which averaged four hundred voices and enrolled one thousand during the season. He was Dean of the College of Music in which Wm. H. Sherwood, Bernhard Listemann, Wheeler, Flagler, and Leason were teachers. Dr. Palmer gave his personal attention to the department of methods, analytical harmony, teachers and conducting clubs and to the big choir. Thousands were attracted to Chautauqua, N. Y., annually by the masterful rendering of music by the great choir under the direction of Dr. Palmer. The vast amphitheatre often failed to accommodate the crowds that attended the concerts and sacred song services and hundreds could be seen standing through an entire program. There is no one man in his field of labor who has stood professionally in the presence of so many people. His usefulness extended from ocean to ocean, and from the Gulf to the British possessions.

His most helpful influences on daily life have unquestionably been exerted through his sacred music. He has been called the poet-musician since he has in so many instances written both the words and music of his popular pieces. Among these are his useful and widely known hymns : " Yield Not to Temptation," " Shall I Let Him In," " Beautiful Home," "The Rose of Sharon," " Step by Step," " Jesus Loves Little Children," etc., all of which he has set to appropriate music. Space would fail us to mention all of his sacred songs. Everybody has sung his " Galilee, Blue Galilee," " Peace, Be Still," " Come, Sinner Come," " By and By We Shall Meet Him," " Life's Balance Sheet," etc. Some of his hymns are sung the world over wherever the Christian religion is found, having been translated into numerous tongues. His never dying "Yield Not to Temptation" has been printed millions of times.

"The sun never sets" on the lands that use his verse and song. He has also issued many sheet songs that have had wide circulation. "She Sleeps in the Valley so Sweet," "Fawn Footed Nannie," etc.

In Chicago he edited and published for years a musical monthly, called the *Concordia*. His first two books were "The Song Queen" and "Song King." They had immense sales. Among his theoretical works are his "Theory of Music," "Class Method," "Manual for Teachers," "Brief Statements," "Musical Catechism," "Piano Primer," "Dictionary of Musical Terms," etc., etc., all of which are standard, being used by the best teachers and music schools. They too have had enormous sales. His theoretical writing is characterized by clearness and accuracy, and his music is distinguished for grace, purity and melodiousness.

A large number of Dr. Palmer's books, collections of songs of all grades, always containing the best of music, are to-day being used in schools and churches everywhere in this country. He wrote and compiled fifty volumes in the interest of music. In recognition of the great services rendered in the West by the introduction of thorough methods and high grades of music, the Chicago University conferred upon him the honorable degree of Doctor of Music, and a year later, for similar services rendered in the East, the Alfred University conferred upon him the same degree.

As a leader Dr. Palmer was an inspiration to any choir or chorus and was not surpassed in kindly thought and skill. He had enthusiasm that was contagious and was also blessed with the staying quality and the genius of good fellowship. Dr. Palmer conducted the Chautauqua, N. Y., Chorus for fourteen years, built up the choir at the Broom Street Tabernacle and had charge of the three choirs for eleven years. He served two church choirs seven years each, worked in the Madison, Wis., Assembly seven years and in the De Funiack Springs, Fla., six years. He was the first leader at the Albany Georgia Assembly and conducted the chorus for a number of years. He served the Cortland, N. Y., Festival nineteen times. The list of festivals in which he worked from two to ten years is too long to mention here.

Dr. Palmer once told an interesting anecdote of his forty-third birthday. He happened on that day to be in London. He said he never had thought about getting old or having to lay aside the work he loved so much; but that day he was struck with the idea that he was old and would be getting older—past his days of usefulness. Soon he would be fifty-three, then sixty-three. The thought was so impressed on him that he felt very gloomy. In the afternoon he went around to hear Spurgeon. The great preacher was exactly Dr. Palmer's age, and listening to the words that fell from those immortal lips, realizing the wonderful power for good that Spurgeon exerted then, and would exert for years to come, it was borne in on him that forty-three was not old; that a world of usefulness still lay before him; that if one's life is filled with love and work, there is no time for age to creep in.

During their visit to the Holy Land Dr. and Mrs. Palmer were invited to a Sunday afternoon tea in Jerusalem, and were greeted by about fifty people who sat at the same table.   Instead of saying " Grace " all joined in singing his

> " By and by we shall meet Him,
> By and by we shall greet Him."

When at Tiberias on the Sea of Galilee, the young people of the mission invited the Doctor to a moonlight row on the sea and surprised him by singing his "Galilee, Blue Galilee " and " Peace, Be Still " on the beautiful waters which gave rise to the songs.

When returning from Nazareth to Jerusalem, Dr. Palmer was invited to spend a night at the mission in Nablous (the old Shechem of Bible times).   The medical missionary, the Rev. Dr. Fallsheer who has a church consisting of about two hundred converted Mohammedans, had arranged a meeting that night and asked Dr. Palmer to play the organ during the service which was conducted entirely in the Arabic language.   As the Arabic reads from right to left instead of from left to right as in English, the music must conform to that plan, *i. e.*, it begins at the extreme right and is read to the left, so the Doctor had to play backwards, so to say, through the entire service, during which his hymn " Yield Not to Temptation " was sung in Arabic by the congregation.

He was well known on the lecture platform of many states in connection with subjects other than musical. He has devoted much time to astronomy and gave his lecture on this subject with all the charm that belongs to only a true lover of the science.   Again he was eagerly sought as a lecturer to give his illustrated lectures on the Orient and the Holy Land.   He has carried into these other lines the same quick brain and forceful activity that developed his music work years ago and placed him in its first ranks.

Dr. Palmer owned a beautiful home at Park Hill-on-Hudson. From two windows in his study there is an extended view of the river and Palisades. This view was always a great joy to him. He was also fond of the trees, flowering shrubs, and plants. He would go out before breakfast looking for new buds and blossoms. There is a symmetrical young maple tree standing on the summit of the grounds that he took delight in showing to callers and visitors. It has always been called Dr. Palmer's tree.

Dr. Palmer's last public services were done in the Mountain Summer Assembly at Ebensburg, Pa., in 1907. He closed with a fine concert the first of August.

In the autumn when a purple haze softened the sunlight and a wealth of autumn leaves had colored the Palisades and crept up the hillside Dr. Palmer passed peacefully to rest in the home he loved, November 15, 1907, in the seventy-third year of his age.

L. C. AND DR. A. B. EVERETT.

XIV

L. C. and Dr. A. B. Everett

THE Everetts and McIntosh were to the music of the South what Mason, Hastings, Bradbury and others were to the music of the North.

It is greatly to be regretted that the records we have of the lives of the Everetts are so meagre. Strange to say, and strange as it may seem, there was but little record kept of the work and lives of these great men of the southland. Perhaps this was due largely to the undeveloped condition of the South in that day. Also because the Civil War "broke out," when they were in the very height of musical glory. Seemingly they had no thought of a future history to record the achievements of the past. They labored under many disadvantages which all pioneers have to encounter. However, their seed sowing was by no means a vain thing.

As these two brothers, L. C. and A. B. Everett, were so closely and intimately connected in their life-work, we give a joint sketch of them. Their brothers B. H. and N. E. Everett were also good musicians, but their work was not so pronounced as that of the subjects of this sketch.

L. C. Everett was born in Virginia in 1818 ; died in Elmira, N. Y., in April, 1867, while on his return from Europe.

Asa Brooks Everett was born in Virginia in 1828 ; died near Nashville, Tenn., in September, 1875.

In early manhood they were broadly and liberally educated, the one for the Christian ministry and the other for the practice of medicine.   During this time Mr. L. C. Everett gave much attention to the study of church music, believing it would be valuable to him in his chosen work as a minister of the Gospel.   His example influenced his younger brother, and together they pursued their studies and investigations of the subject.   Being passionately fond of music, they became intensely interested and finally decided to forego their original purposes and to adopt music as their profession.

On the strength of this decision they went to Boston, and took a pretty thorough course of musical instruction. They also attended some normal musical institutes of the day.   Returning South they began teaching vocal music in classes and soon became famous.   Being desirous of still further musical study, Dr. A. B. Everett went to Leipzig, Germany, and took a four years' course.   He then returned to America and joined his brother in an effort to develop an easy practical and scientific method of elementary class instruction.   " The Everett System " was the final outcome, and was exceedingly popular in its day.

The L. C. Everett Co., which consisted of L. C. and A. B. Everett, and R. M. McIntosh, had prior to the Civil War in their employ over fifty teachers of vocal music in the Southern and Middle Atlantic states, who had received an individual normal training under them for a period of two months.   They paid each teacher a salary of one hundred dollars per month and expenses.

The Everetts were prolific and popular writers of church music.

For a time they made Richmond, Va., their headquarters. Later the Everett family moved to Pennsylvania. As Prof. L. C. Everett passed away before the gospel song period, a few of his most popular hymn tunes are mentioned : " Bealoth," " Spring," " Mattie," " Beaufort," " Schumann," " Solitude," and " Wyanet." He also composed many anthems.

Dr. A. B. Everett composed many excellent hymn tunes and anthems, and devoted the latter years of his life almost entirely to writing gospel songs. The following are considered among his most popular : " Footsteps of Jesus," " Knocking at the Door," " Come Unto Me," " To that City Will You Go ? " " Hear Him Calling," and " Summer Land." They edited several valuable collections of music.

Prof. L. C. Everett's largest and most popular collection was " The Wesleyan Hymn and Tune Book," published by the Publishing House of the M. E. Church South.

Dr. A. B. Everett's largest and most important book was " The Sceptre," published by The Biglow & Main Co., New York.

Dr. R. M. McIntosh, their pupil and also associate until the Civil War, had from the beginning of his editorial work full access to the Everett copyrights and finally became the owner of them ; consequently the Everetts' music, including hymn tunes, anthems and gospel songs, have occupied a permanent place in all the collections edited by him, and later, the hymnals and gospel song books edited by Prof. H. R. Christie. Their music has also appeared in many books edited by other authors. Prof. L. C. Everett was a member of the M. E. Church South, and Dr. A. B. Everett a communicant of the Christian Church.

The musical impress left on the South by their labors is an honored and abiding monument to the Everetts.

R. M. McINTOSH.

XV

Dr. R. M. McIntosh

RIGDON McCOY McINTOSH was born in Maury County, Tenn., April 3, 1836. His musical gifts as well as a bright, cheerful temperament were the direct inheritance from his mother, Mrs. Mamie (Biggs) McIntosh. He often expressed great faith in his Scotch father, Hector McIntosh. He considered it a good beginning in life to have been born on a farm and reared with a goodly number of brothers and sisters.

He was educated at Jackson College, Columbia, Tenn. After leaving college he was for a time professor of English and Mathematics in Triam Alabama High School.

In early manhood, the seeming chance acquaintance of the Everett brothers changed the whole course of his after life. Previous to this he had not thought of music as a profession, but rather that of law. He took a special course of musical instruction under L. C. and A. B. Everett. Then for a number of years he worked with them, teaching, composing and editing books.

His work led him to Farmville, Va., and while there he married Miss Sallie McClasson. His wife's estate became his home until after the birth of his two children, Loulie Everett and Nannie. His marriage with a pure Christian woman brought another influence to bear on the life of this gifted man. Through her

consecrated life and the guidance of the Holy Spirit,
he became a Christian and united with the M. E.
Church South. Ever afterwards his gift of song was
dedicated to the Master's use.

In 1875 he was elected principal of the music department of the Vanderbilt University, Nashville,
Tenn. His composition, "Vanderbilt's Ode," was
sung and used at the laying of the corner-stone of the
first one of the university buildings.

In 1877 he accepted the position of Professor of
Music in Emory College, Oxford, Ga. This institution
conferred on him the degree of Music Doctor. Oxford
became his permanent home, and he served as Mayor
for a number of years.

He finally established The R. M. McIntosh Publishing Company, and in 1895 severed his connection with
Emory College and devoted his time exclusively to the
company.

Dr. McIntosh's church collections are: "Tabor,"
"Herman," "Methodist Hymn and Tune Book,"
"Prayer and Praise," "Christian Hymns," "Gospel
Grace," and "McIntosh's Anthems."

Sunday-school books: "Glad Tidings," "Amaranth,"
"Emerald," "The Gem," "Good News," "Light and
Life," "New Life, No. 1," "New Life, No. 2," "Living
Songs," "Pure Words," and "Songs of Service."
H. R. Christie was co-editor of the last two books men-
tioned.

Class Books and Periodicals: "McIntosh's Musical
Notation," "The Everett-McIntosh Method of Teaching Musical Notation," and "Elementary Vocal Music
in Classes," "McIntosh's Class and Chorus Book,"
"The Musical Worker."

The "Tabor," "Amaranth" and "New Life, No. 1," have had the largest sales, two of these reaching the two million mark. The aggregate sales of all his books is nearly six and a half million copies.

Among the many popular gospel songs which he composed, we mention the following: "The Wise Virgins," "At the Beautiful Gate," "Tell It Again," "Not Far From the Kingdom," "Gathering Home," "The Kingdom Coming," "For Many, Many Years," "Story of the Cross."

Dr. McIntosh was music editor of the Publishing House of the Methodist Episcopal Church South for over thirty years and this house published most of his books. Oliver Ditson Company, Boston, Mass., published "Good News," "Light and Life," and "McIntosh's Anthems"; J. W. Burke & Co., Macon, Ga., "McIntosh's Class and Chorus Book," and The Gospel Advocate Co., Nashville, Tenn., "Christian Hymns."

As a teacher he was gifted in a remarkable degree, as those who studied under him testify. His method was peculiarly his own, and was fruitful in the best of results. He was a busy teacher and his services were in great demand.

As a vocalist, his voice was pure and sympathetic, and when leading a large chorus was very powerful. He was a fine director of choruses—a favorite throughout all the South.

Frederick N. Crouch, author of "Kathleen Mavourneen," said in *Southern Opinion*, in a review of Dr. McIntosh's work in Richmond, Va., "I have heard John Hullah before his great chorus in London and Dr. Lowell Mason before his old Handel and Haydn Society in Boston, but I never heard Professor McIntosh's equal on the teacher's rostrum, nor any one who could approach him as a master in chorus drill. At first, when the members of his old Richmond Society of Music were lauding him to the skies, I could not believe in him. Finally I slipped into his lecture room one night, and next into his chorus drill room, night after night. He does not know me now, but all I have said of him is the truth; and if I know nothing else in the world I know a drill master when I see him. The members of his chorus do not overestimate him."

His hymn tunes, anthems, gospel songs and books speak for themselves as to his ability as a composer and editor. His songs have not alone found a place in the hearts of the people North and South, but a number of them have been translated into different languages and sung by missionaries in many foreign lands.

Great efforts were made by prominent evangelists to procure his services for the evangelistic field; but he was unwilling to sever his connections with the Publishing House of the M. E. Church South and educational institutions for this field of labor. However he did sing for some important meetings, among which was Rev. Sam P. Jones' meeting held for Talmage's Church, Brooklyn, N. Y., and the Annual and General Conferences of the M. E. Church South. One friend in writing of him says: "Dr. McIntosh had many strong and noble characteristics, and made lasting friends of the most deserving men with whom he came in contact." Another speaking of him says: "Few if any had a stronger devotion for his family and friends."

His compositions in the treatment of hymns of the future life were full of pathos and power and it was a touching coincidence that on that dark, sad night, while he lay in an upper room dying, an unknown youth, unconscious of the death scene within, passed wearily homeward whistling as he went:

> " Up to the bountiful Giver of life,
>   Gathering home ! gathering home,"

and thus the Asaph fell asleep as the notes of his own song were echoing around him on the earthward side and floating out across the mystical stream to mingle with the melodies of a divine minstrelsy on the farther shore.

Dr. R. M. McIntosh died July 2, 1899, at the residence of his daughter, Mrs. E. T. Burns, Atlanta, Ga., and was interred July 4th in the cemetery at Oxford, Ga. Only his own songs were sung at the funeral service. With his brethren, Andrew, Few, Meane and Haygood he sleeps as he lived and labored—among his own people.

H. R. CHRISTIE.

XVI

H. R. Christie

THE subject of this sketch, Harvey Robert Christie, was born in Monroe County, W. Va., June 29, 1848, and is of English and Scotch-Irish descent. His great grandfather, James Christie, who came from London, was a Methodist minister, and was instrumental in erecting Rehoboth Church in 1785, the first in the country. His father, James Maxwell Christie, and his mother, Cynthia Peters (Clark) Christie, were members of the Methodist Church. They had eleven children born to them, three daughters and eight sons, of whom seven survive.

In 1859 the family removed to Mercer County. Here for the first time they came in contact with the people designated as the Disciples of Christ and had frequent opportunities to hear the Gospel preached with power by such faithful ministers as Duncan, Cowgill, Bullard, Baber, Lucas and others. This resulted in a change of their church relationship. In 1869 they united with the Christian Church and all the children followed their example.

Young Christie received his first literary training in the public schools, and was subsequently liberally educated at the seminary.

He began to teach singing classes in 1871 and continued until 1874. His success up to this time justified him in making music his profession. This decision caused him to seek a higher course of study and a better method of instruction. To accomplish his purpose thoroughly, he entered a course of training under Prof. R. M. McIntosh, who was at that time principal of the music department of the Vanderbilt University.

He remained in Tennessee until June, 1876. During this period he taught quite a number of classes in Sumner, Wilson and Davidson Counties. Returning to West Virginia he continued his class teaching until April, 1877. At this time he opened his first normal session—two months at the Concord State Normal School, Athens, W. Va. This he followed with a similar session at Princeton, W. Va. The next normal was held at Rural Retreat, Va., in 1878, and four sessions were held at Snowville, Va., during the years 1879–1880. In 1881 he opened a nine-months' session at Rural Retreat. During this year he decided to add a business department, and he entered the Commercial College of Kentucky University. In 1882 he removed to Milligan College, Tennessee, where he became one of the donors of the college and has since been a permanent member of the Board of Directors.

The school under the name of Christie's Music and Commercial Institute, had a liberal patronage until 1884, when Washington College, Tennessee, offered greater inducements and the institution was removed and merged into Christie's Music and Business College.

There were full courses of study offered in both the music and commercial departments of this school under a corps of competent instructors. Various musical organizations, both vocal and instrumental, were connected with the institute. The school continued for a period of eight years.

Nearly every year, in addition to the regular session, a summer term was held at the State Normal School, Athens, W. Va. The largest annual enrollment including all departments was 384 students representing twenty-six states. Of this number 116 were instrumental pupils.

It might be interesting to note that Charles M. Alexander, the renowned singing evangelist, was a pupil in this school. Professor Christie is quite a successful teacher and organizer. Dr. R. M. McIntosh in writing of him says : " I regard Prof. H. R. Christie one of the best teachers I ever knew, and he has had much to do with the training of the people of his own state and elsewhere. He is acknowledged by all who know him to be a man of superior judgment, taste and skill in all the departments of church and Sunday-school music."

He resides at Willowton, W. Va.

In 1894 he became editor of the musical department of The Standard Publishing Company, Cincinnati, Ohio, one of the leading publishing houses of the Christian Church.

Professor Christie's books show purpose and the treatment of subjects is systematic in every detail. In 1876 he edited " Favorite Songs " (his brother T. H. R. assisting him) for the benefit of teachers. This book proved to be quite popular with the profession. In 1892 he assisted R. M. McIntosh in editing " Words of Truth," a book for Sunday-schools.

In 1893 he went to Oxford, Ga., and spent two years. While there he occupied the office of Dr. McIntosh where he had full access to his musical library as well as his assistance in the further study of hymnology, musical authors and their works.

During this time he edited " Gospel Light," a church hymnal of 432 pages. He claims this was the first church hymnal in which all the words were printed in the score with the music.

In 1896 he assisted R. M. McIntosh in editing " Songs of Service," for young people's meetings. In 1906 he edited " The Christian Church Hymnal," a book of 432 pages. This collection has 169 Responsive Bible Readings—prepared by M. M. Davis, Dallas, Texas.

His new (1911) book, " Songs of Evangelism," contains many of the most famous gospel songs and is preeminently a book for the purposes intended. Among his best compositions may be mentioned : " What Have I Done To-day ? " " He Knows it All," " Let Him Come In," " Let it Shine in Your Soul," " I Shall Have Stars in My Crown," " Hear the Call," " Freely Give," " Ambassadors for Christ," and " A Call Comes Ringing to Me."

Professor Christie is an able director of congregational singing, choirs, evangelistic meetings, conventions and other assemblies.

His books are having immense sales and may be found in every state in the Union, and in various foreign countries.

" O give thanks unto the Lord ; for He is good. Sing praises unto His name ; for it is pleasant."

REV. ISAIAH BALTZELL.

XVII

Rev. Isaiah Baltzell

IT is something worthy of note that a man should have been a pioneer in any line. Such is the record of the musical work of Rev. Isaiah Baltzell who was one of the first, and for a considerable period one of the foremost writers of Sunday-school and revival music in the United Brethren Church. Through long years of faithful service his influence upon the musical work of the denomination with which he was connected was powerful.

He was born near Frederick City, Md., November 26, 1832, his father, a farmer, whose family trace goes back through Kentucky and Tennessee to those sturdy colonists of German blood who came to North Carolina before the Revolution. His mother was of the Pennsylvania German stock who had built up Southern Pennsylvania and Northern Maryland.

His education was limited to the opportunities offered by the common schools of his neighborhood, and to several terms at a private school conducted under the auspices of the Moravian Church, at Graceham, in the county in which he was born. While he was still a lad his parents moved to the neighborhood of Mechanicstown (now Thurmont), Md., where he was converted at a camp-meeting held by the United Brethren. He became a member of that organization, and later, through his influence, his parents, both of them members of the Lutheran faith, and his brothers and sisters, also identified themselves with the United Brethren.

While still in his teens he felt a call to the ministry and in 1850 was ordained at Edinburg, Va., and assigned to a circuit in the eastern part of the present state of West Virginia. He served several charges in this section, and after his marriage to Miss Cecilia Caroline James, at Mount Jackson, Va., he was sent to Baltimore, as pastor of a congregation which he built up from a mission to a self-sustaining body. From Baltimore he went again to Western Maryland, serving as pastor at Myerstown, and Boonsboro, with a short stay at Shiremanstown, Pa. This was during the Civil War period. At the close of the war he went to Hagerstown, Md., and then returned to Pennsylvania, where he remained for the rest of his life, filling pastorates at New Holland, and Mountville, Lancaster County, and at Highspire, Dauphin County, Harrisburg and Reading. During this period he served a number of years as Presiding Elder of one of the districts of the East Pennsylvania Conference, and as delegate to the General Conference of the Church and Educational Board. At the time of his death, January 16, 1893, he was engaged in raising funds to build a church at Pottstown, Pa.

He left a widow and three children, two of whom are engaged in musical work : Winton J., editor of the *Musician*, published by the Oliver Ditson Company, Boston ; composer of songs and anthems, and author of a successful history of music and a biographical dictionary of musicians ; Margaret A., teacher in a conservatory of music, at Reading, Pa.

Even as a boy Isaiah Baltzell was marked out as

having more than ordinary talent for music ; he loved
to sing and long before he learned the rudiments of
music, tried to write little tunes.   As a young minister
he was popular and successful owing to his ability to
sing, to lead a congregation and to teach others to
sing.   He frequently conducted singing schools on his
various charges.

The first book that he published was a small collection known as the " Revival Songster," issued at Balti-
more, in 1859.   The next was a little pamphlet called
" Choral Gems," published in 1871, in which collection
he was assisted by the Rev. G. W. M. Rigor.   His
books now began to follow in quick succession ; among
the most popular are : " Camp Meeting Singer,"
" Golden Songs," " Rippling Rills," " Heavenly Carols,"
" Gates of Praise," " Songs of Cheer," " Songs of
Grace," " Songs of the Kingdom," " Holy Voices,"
" Notes of Triumph," " Songs of Refreshing," " Garnered
Sheaves," and " The Master's Praise."   Mr. E. S.
Lorenz was associated with Mr. Baltzell in editing
several of these books.   Among his most popular songs
are : " No Room in Heaven," " Good News Comes O'er
the Sea," " Some Mother's Child," " Take my Heart,
Dear Jesus," " I Want to be a Worker," and " Go,
Wash in the Stream."

Rev. Isaiah Baltzell's life was one filled with good
works ; his labors of love and song will go on and continue to inspire hearts to nobler aspirations.

PHILIP PHILLIPS.

XVIII

Philip Phillips

"THE SINGING PILGRIM," as Mr. Phillips was generally called and familiarly known, was born August 13, 1834, in Chautauqua County, N. Y. He was a "boy on a farm" in early life; but he had a talent for music and a good tenor voice for performing it. Mr. Phillips began teaching singing school at the age of nineteen, and met with great success. In 1858, while teaching singing classes in Marion, Ohio, he met the lady of his choice in the person of Miss Olive M. Clark. They were married the following year. He began his active business life in 1860, the year after his marriage, when he formed a partnership with Wm. Sumner & Co., under the firm name of Philip Phillips & Co., for the sale of pianos and organs and the publication of Sunday-school singing books, at Cincinnati, O. In the sale of instruments he was remarkably successful, though in competition with a number of well-established firms. Mr. Phillips frequently introduced himself into a village or city by placing a melodeon in some vehicle and locating himself and outfit on some prominent street-corner, and then begin to sing and play. It is needless to say that his marvellous voice would draw the crowds, and under its magic charm they would buy his books and give him orders for instruments. Indeed his great success in this direction, with a very limited financial capital, was one of the inducements which led Wm. Sumner & Co., already occupying several states with sewing-machine agencies, with headquarters at Cincinnati, to aid him with all the capital he might need for his business, and let him have the greater portion of the magnificent room they were occupying in Pike's former Opera House, for the display and sale of his wares. In the composition and sale of Sunday-school song books Mr. Phillips had, at that time, but few competitors; the principal one being W. B. Bradbury, although Horace Waters, of New York, and a few others were in the field, but not occupying it. But Mr. Phillips and Mr. Bradbury were friends rather than competitors, and this friendship continued unbroken through life.

The first book issued by him was " Early Blossoms," which was followed by " Musical Leaves." This was published in three parts and afterwards consolidated into one volume. The sales of this book aggregated about three-quarters of a million copies, and was probably the most popular of all his books in the West.

The burning of Pike's Opera House, in 1865, destroyed the entire stock of Philip Phillips & Co., and although with the insurance received the stock was partly replenished and the business transferred to another location in the city, yet they did not recover the lost trade, and in 1867 Mr. Phillips transferred his headquarters to New York City, where they remained until his death. When he left for New York he had about ready for publication his " Singing Pilgrim," and shortly after his arrival in the city he issued the book. It proved immensely popular in every section of the United States, but more especially in the East, while it outrivalled its successful predecessor in the West. Subsequently he edited or published the following and in the order here given, viz.: "Song Life," "Song Sermons," "New Hymn and Tune Book," "Hallowed Songs," "American Sacred Songster," "Home Songs," "Temperance Songs," "Standard Gems," "Colonial Singer," "International Song Service," and "Our New Hymnal," of which the "American Sacred Songster," issued in Great Britain, attained a sale of over one million. By the year 1868 the story of his success and popularity as a singer and composer had reached foreign countries, and in that year the London Sunday School Association invited him to give one hundred evenings of sacred song in that city and the United Kingdom, for which they agreed to give him a liberal compensation. He accepted it, made the tour, and returned to his native country with additional laurels. A few years later, on invitation, he made another similar visit and was everywhere received with unbounded enthusiasm.

In 1875 an urgent invitation, accompanied with a pledge of a handsome remuneration for his services, besides an ample sum for expenses of himself and family—a wife and two sons—he left San Francisco for Australia, where he conducted one hundred song services. He returned to New York in two years, singing en route at Ceylon, in India, Japan, Jerusalem, Egypt, Italy, and various places in the continent of Europe and in England, where he tarried long enough to give two hundred "song services." Having previously sung at numerous places between New York and San Francisco, this last trip belted the world, and the most remarkable feature of this "belting" was that he returned to New York without missing any engagement in the entire circle of song. During this trip he had numberless delightful experiencies, but the opportunity which he had and embraced of singing in the "Church of the Nativity," in Bethlehem, he always regarded as the greatest privilege of his life.

The following is a summary of the song services which Mr. Phillips held : " Great Britain and Ireland, 972 ; Continental Europe, 150 ; Canada and Australia, 187 ; India, Palestine and Egypt, 81 ; United States, 3,200. It is estimated that he has given in all nearly 4,000 services for benevolent purposes, exclusively, which netted for various worthy charities over $112,000."

He was a deeply pious man, and his songs went to the hearts of his hearers with happiest effect.

Mr. Phillips' book entitled, "Round the World with Descriptive Songs," is one of rare excellence.

His warm moral nature and his phenomenal voice were the two keys which opened up from time to time the avenues to his success. They led primarily to his business partnership in Cincinnati, and to his famous début in public, in 1865, at a vast meeting held in Washington, D. C., in the interest of the Christian Commission. This meeting was presided over by Secretary Seward, was attended by President Lincoln and other distinguished men. A great singer, well known in musical circles, had been duly advertised to be present, was present and sang. Mr. Stuart, the president of the Commission, had heard Mr. Phillips sing and invited him to be present. During the meeting he invited him to sing and he responded with " Your Mission." The song, the singer, the cause and the audience were all *en rapport* and the effect was magical.

This drew out from President Lincoln, written on a scrap of program, the request for Mr. Phillips to repeat his song " Your Mission " ; and Mr. Phillips, having gone into the meeting a comparative stranger, went out with a name to be heralded throughout the world.   The other singer, who went in with éclat, sang grandly to the head and was forgotten ; the other sang to the heart and was immortalized.   His voice was the magnet that drew the masses, and his sweet moral nature the tendrils that bound them to him.

Philip Phillips died at Delaware, Ohio, June 25, 1895.   He left one son.

T. M. TOWNE.

XIX

T. Martin Towne

T. MARTIN TOWNE was born in the little romantic, hilly town of Coleraine, Franklin County, Mass., May 31, 1835. This county is distinguished as the birthplace of a number of celebrated musicians—Clarence Eddy, W. F. Sherwin, and others. Mr. Towne has been heard to say that "it is a good county to be born in, and a good one to emigrate from."

He was brought up on a farm, attended district school and the old-fashioned singing school, where he first commenced to study the rudiments of music. He, however, gives the most credit to his father, Dea Arid Towne, for his advancement. It was he that inspired the boy to persevere in gaining the mastery over the difficulties of reading music at sight. When seventeen years of age he attended Williston's Seminary at East Hampton, Mass. Here he was under the instruction of Professor Nason, and gained the complete mastery of all difficult rhythmic forms and syncopation. Professor Nason gave him much encouragement and advised him to study in Germany, and fit himself for a teacher.

When twenty years of age he attended a musical convention at Shelburne, Mass., under the direction of the late Prof. W. F. Sherwin. Mr. Sherwin made a proposition to Mr. Towne to study with him and pay for his tuition in vocal and instrumental music by singing in his choir and club. He accepted and removed to Hudson, N. Y., where he studied two years the pianoforte, singing and pedagogics. He then removed to Albany, and accepted a position in St. Peter's Protestant Episcopal Church as tenor, in a quartet choir. He afterwards held the same position in Dr. Ray Palmer's church (author of " My Faith Looks Up to Thee "); while in Albany he was the leading tenor of that city.

After four years of preparation he left to go west and grow up with the country. He commenced teaching in Ypsilanti, Mich., but at the end of a year was called to Detroit to conduct a singing society and teach vocal music in the public schools, being the first teacher to be employed by the Board of Education to teach that branch. During these years he attended a normal music school at North Reading, Mass., and studied with Dr. Lowell Mason, Geo. F. Root and Wm. B. Bradbury. He cherishes to this day the letters and words of recommendation he received from these eminent teachers, and the inspiration and culture that came through mingling with so many prominent and talented students.

Early during the war Mr. Towne resigned as teacher in the public schools and for a year sang with the old Continental Vocalists. While with them he had a fine opportunity of ascertaining the taste of the people in music and learned the art of composing and arranging to please the masses. His first published song was " Gentle Be Thy Footfall." This manuscript he gave to Mr. S. Brainard, of Cleveland, who published it. After several years Mr. Brainard presented the author with fifty copies of it, saying that it had sold very well. Mr. Towne finally settled in Janesville, Wis., where he taught one year and then enlisted in the fortieth regiment of infantry. He was appointed principal musician of the regiment and served until mustered out. After this he was called to Milwaukee to teach vocal music in the Female College and sing in Plymouth Church. He held those positions two years and composed many songs and quartets. He then removed to Chicago, where he has since lived.

Since going to Chicago he has been very busy leading large choirs, holding conventions, and composing. He has taught much in summer normals, and is a strong believer in such schools. He was one of the teachers in the famous normal school held at South Bend, Ind., in 1870. This was the most successful school of the kind ever held; it was managed by Dr. Geo. F. Root. At this school Mr. Towne taught the sopranos in voice culture; P. P. Bliss the basses; Prof. O. Blackman the altos; Carlo Bassini gave the teachers lessons in classes by themselves and superintended them in their individual work. Mr. Towne also taught one of the harmony classes and sang part of the tenor solos in the " Creation " at the closing concert. The faculty studied harmony under Dr. William Mason. Mr. Towne remembers these lessons with much pleasure. The time was largely spent in the study of the diminished seventh chord—its character and various resolutions. The Doctor sometimes complimented our friend on the way he worked out his exercises, but one day, after playing a tune through, he said nothing, and Mr. Towne asked if there were any mistakes. The Doctor replied as follows: "No, it is free from errors, but *there is no character in it.*" This opened Mr. Towne's eyes, and ever since then he has tried in his compositions to compose music with character in it. He endeavors to wed music to the sentiment expressed in the words, and at the same time not to write so difficult as to debar ordinary singers from using it. He believes that the strength of music is not alone in the harmony, but in the harmony and melody combined.

Mr. Towne's compositions are very numerous and varied; he composes Sunday-school songs, gospel songs, hymn tunes, anthems, ballads, glees, quartets, cantatas, and dramatic pieces with equal facility. He has cantatas for Christmas, Children's Day, Harvest Home, Easter, missionary concerts, school exhibitions, temperance, etc., some forty in all, and they are having large sales. "Lost and Saved" (for temperance) has had no competitor in this country and is yet being given all over the United States.

Among his most popular books are "The Cluster," "Good Will," "Sabbath Songs," "Church and Prayer Meeting Songs," "Temperance Anthems," "Band of Hope Songs," "Choir Anthems," and "Anthems of Joy," with Mr. Straub associate.

He has composed hundreds of sheet songs, duets, and quartets.

Mr. Towne has been the musical editor for the enterprising Sunday-school publishing house of David C. Cook, Chicago, for thirty years, and considerable of his time is given to that firm; not only as musical editor, but in the way of contributing articles on music and primary teaching in Sunday-schools. He has occasionally written for denominational church papers on congregational music and kindred topics.

He has a pleasant home in Chicago. His wife, Mrs. Belle Kellogg Towne, is the well-known writer for the young, and for many years has been the managing editor for David C. Cook's papers—*The Young People's Weekly*, *The Weekly Welcome* and *The Girl's Companion*. She is author of several books. Mr. and Mrs. Towne are members of the M. E. Church and are active in church work.

WM. G. FISCHER.

XX

William G. Fischer

WILLIAM G. FISCHER was born in Baltimore, Md., October 14, 1835. His father was from Wurtemburg, Germany. He developed as a child his inclination towards music, and, at the age of eight, would start the singing in a German church in Baltimore. He learned to read music in a church singing class, and afterwards studied harmony, piano and organ, under the best of teachers. He learned the book-binding trade at J. B. Lippincott's, in Philadelphia; and spent his evenings studying and practicing music. He had much experience in training and leading large bodies of singers of all ages; was much sought after to lead choirs and choruses in sacred music in Philadelphia, and in the meantime taught singing, piano and the theory of music.

Mr. Fischer has been closely connected with the Welsh in their musical festivals, and directed the combined Welsh Societies at the Bi-Centennial of the landing of William Penn.

In 1858 he was elected Professor of Music at Girard College, and resigned in 1868, after ten happy years. The committee showed their appreciation of him and their confidence in him by requesting him to name his successor. Before leaving Girard College he started in the piano business, where he built up one of the most prosperous piano houses in the country. He went into partnership with Mr. J. E. Gould, a partnership which was only dissolved by the death of Mr. Gould in 1875. From that time Mr. Fischer was sole proprietor of the large business house for a number of years, when he took his oldest son, Charles, into partnership, and finally retired in 1898, being succeeded by his son.

While Mr. Fischer is well known in business circles, also as a teacher and leader of choirs and choruses, he is, perhaps, best known as a composer of gospel songs, many of which have been sung wherever the Gospel has been preached. He was often urged to write and publish books of sacred music, but in this he seemed to have but little ambition, and has contented himself by writing and supplying others. His music may be found in all of the standard hymnals.

Among the most popular of his hymns are the following : "I Love to Tell the Story," "Whiter than Snow," "I am Trusting, Lord, in Thee," "A Little Talk with Jesus," "O, 'Twas Love, Wondrous Love," "Waiting at the Pool," "Valley of Blessing," and many others that have largely influenced burdened souls towards the higher and better life. Mr. Fischer's gospel songs are characterized by a distinctive devotional ring.

He resides in Philadelphia, and is a highly respected Christian gentleman. While he is well advanced in years, we hope he may still be able to contribute of the genius of his soul in gospel song.

NOTE.—Since the above sketch was written, Mr. Wm. G. Fischer passed to his reward, which occurred August 13, 1912. He was a good man and he loved to " Tell the Story " of Him who can make us " Whiter than Snow."

THEO. F. SEWARD.

XXI

Theodore Frelinghuysen Seward

THE subject of our sketch came from a distinguished family, Wm. H. Seward, Secretary of State in the Lincoln administration, being a second cousin.

Theodore F. Seward was born in Florida, N. Y., January 25, 1835, and his boyhood days were spent in his native town. His education was gained in the institute at Florida, endowed by Judge Seward, a relative. Later he attended the Normal Musical Institute at North Reading, near Boston, Mass., where he took several courses in musical training, studying with Lowell Mason, Geo. F. Root, and Thomas F. Hastings. While at this institute he started on the path which led him to his later notable achievement. He loved musical work, and adopted it as his life's vocation. He became professor in the Teachers' College in New York, where he soon demonstrated his aptness for imparting his knowledge of this art to those under his charge. This institution was later merged into Columbia University.

While living in Rochester, N. Y., Professor Seward married Miss Mary H. Coggeshall, of New London, Conn., on June 12, 1860. From Rochester he moved to Brooklyn, and then to Orange, N. J., going to the latter place in 1868. Before taking up the larger work of his life he was the supervisor of music in the public schools of Orange and contiguous cities, and organist and musical director in several of the churches. He soon achieved national fame as a musical composer, teacher, editor of musical periodicals and author of educational works. He was for many years associated in musical affairs with Dr. Mason, and was co-editor with him of his later musical and educational works.

It is, perhaps, difficult to tell which of his many excellent compositions has gained the most popularity, but the one hymn he loved, and which is sung in all the Protestant Sunday-schools, is one of his best, "Go and Tell Jesus." He introduced the tonic sol-fa system of teaching music which has such vogue in England.

But what he regarded as his most distinctive and interesting musical work was recording and thus preserving many of the religious melodies of the Southern slaves, known as "spirituals," or "slave songs," of which "Swing Low, Sweet Chariot," and "Turn Back, Pharaoh's Army," are types. More than a hundred of these which he collected are published under the title of "Jubilee Songs," by the Biglow & Main Co., of New York City. This work was done in connection with the famous Fisk Jubilee Singers, who raised several hundred thousand dollars by their concerts in America and Europe for their University at Nashville, Tenn. Mr. Seward was musical director and voice trainer for the company during their second European tour.

With the advancing years his kind and lovable nature expanded more and more. New fields of work continually opened up before him. He was the very embodiment of a nature full of sunshine, and his aim through life was to continually infuse as much of love into the human race as possible. In 1891 he organized the Brotherhood of Christian Unity; in 1897 the Don't Worry Club, and in 1901 the Golden Rule Brotherhood.

It is a curious fact that his adoption of the musical calling developed an element of his nature which in time carried him out of the vocation. It was a process of evolution. He transferred his attention from the harmony of music to the harmony of life—individual life and social life in the broadest sense of that word, which necessarily includes the religious element.

Professor Seward had travelled extensively through Europe and the United States, and his well-spent life was rounded out with ripe experiences gained from observation. An interesting incident occurred while Mr. and Mrs. Seward were in London, England, during the Queen's golden jubilee. The great audience assembled at the Crystal Palace, desiring to conclude the exercises with the singing of " God Save the Queen," called upon Professor Seward to lead the singing. Shortly afterwards they attended the exercise of twenty thousand children, their presence being unknown. When it was learned that they were in the hall the children sang one of the Professor's glees, at the conclusion all making a bow.

Among Professor Seward's treasured keepsakes was an Oxford Bible given him in London by D. L. Moody (as a souvenir of aid he gave in the great revival of 1875–1876), in which the above and other eminent names are written.

Among the numerous musical works with which Professor Seward's name is connected as author or editor, the following are some of the most noted: " The Temple Choir," " American Tune Book," " The

Singer," " The Coronation," " Jubilee Songs," " Glee Circle " ; in association with Dr. Lowell Mason, " The Pestalozzian Music Teacher." He also had published a number of tonic sol-fa works.

He was editor of *The New York Musical Pioneer*, 1864 ; *The New York Musical Gazette*, 1867–1873 ; *The Tonic Solfa Advocate*, 1881–1885 ; *Musical Reform*, 1886–1888. Among the religious books written by Professor Seward we mention : " Heaven Every Day," " The School of Life," " Don't Worry ; or, the Scientific Law of Happiness, " " Spiritual Knowing; or, Bible Sunshine," " How to Get Acquainted with God," and many pamphlets and tracts.

Prof. Theo. F. Seward died August 30, 1902, at the home of his daughter, Mrs. Thomas G. Bolles, Orange, N. J.

May his songs and writings continue to throw rays of sunshine in some sad heart.

H. P. MAIN.

XXII

H. P. Main

HUBERT PLATT MAIN, son of Sylvester Main (during his life a member of the firm of Biglow & Main), was born at Ridgefield, Conn., August 17, 1839.

Mr. Main is gifted with a remarkable memory. He remembers distinctly things that occurred as far back as 1842. He hasn't forgotten a whipping received in that year for repeatedly running off from home at evenings to the band room, hiding under the benches and listening to the music.

He attended the district school from 1842 to 1854. His father was an old-fashioned singing-school teacher of unusual skill and success, possessing a fine voice. Hubert began attending his father's singing schools at the age of eleven, although for a time he did not take any interest in anything but the girls. Finally he did give enough attention to observe that the pupils sang one tone for a note that was on a line, and another for the note that was above the line, and still another for a note below the line. He spoke to his father about it, who gave him a few words of explanation, and he immediately began to study the tune " Burton," in the " Dulcimer," and before he went to bed he could read every note of it.

From that time on he practiced reading notes until he could read anything at sight by the syllables—do, re, mi. Wherever he might be he was practicing the do, re, mi's. If when walking on the street any air came to his mind, he would apply the syllables to it, and sing away. He continued to attend singing schools regularly till 1854.

In April of this year he went to New York City and worked as errand boy in a wall paper house. In the fall he returned to Ridgefield for his final winter's schooling. In April of 1855, he became office boy in the piano house of Bristow & Morse. The Bristow of the firm was the now celebrated composer, Geo. F. Bristow. He has ever since been one of Mr. Main's warmest friends.

In June of the same year Mr. Main accepted a position as salesman in a gent's furnishing store, continuing there three years, at the same time playing the melodeon in the Forsyth Street M. E. Church on Sundays. He also attended singing, and devoted all his spare time to music. His first experience in compiling music books was in the year 1855. He helped his father edit the " Sunday School Lute," by I. B. Woodbury.

Mr. Wm. B. Bradbury also sought the assistance of Mr. Main's father in the compilation of his books, commencing with " Cottage Melodies " in 1859, and continuing till his death in 1868. At this time the house of Biglow & Main was formed as successors to the publishing business of Wm. B. Bradbury. During all these years young Main assisted his father in editing the books of Woodbury and Bradbury, in which he was laying the foundation of his own skill, for which he is so well known.

From 1858 to 1864 he was bookkeeper for the piano

house of Hazelton Bros. In November, 1864, he went
to Cincinnati ostensibly as bookkeeper for the piano
house of Philip Phillips & Co., really to arrange his
music for him. After one year he returned to New
York and married. He then connected himself with
the firm of F. J. Huntington & Co., where he was
especially useful on account of his knowledge of the
copyrights of I. B. Woodbury.

In 1866 he assisted Philip Phillips compile the second
M. E. Church Hymn and Tune Book. In fact, he prepared almost all the copy and read all the proofs.

In 1867 he was called to fill a position in the publishing house of Wm. B. Bradbury, New York, and has
remained with Bradbury's successors ever since and is
now treasurer of the company. With but few exceptions, every publication of the house has passed through
his hands in the making, compiling, editing, proof-read-
ing, etc. His acquaintance with Woodbury, Bradbury,
and Thomas J. Cook commenced at the Fairfield
County (Conn.) musical conventions between 1854 and
1861, and later in New York with Theo. E. Perkins,
S. J. Vail, Theo. F. Seward, and others.

He has been a member of all the great choral bodies
of New York, such as the New York Harmonic (1867),
G. F. Bristow, F. L. Ritter, conductors; the Mendelssohn
Union (1869), Theo. Thomas, G. F. Bristow, Otto Singer,
conductors; the Clinton Vocal Union, Newark, N. J.
(1877), B. C. Gregory, conductor; the Newark Harmonic
Society, Dr. L. Damrosch, conductor; also, the Schubert
Society (1881), L. A. Russell, conductor; the New York
Oratorio Society, Dr. L. Damrosch, conductor; the New
York Chorus (1884), Theo. Thomas, conductor.

Mr. Main has attended hundreds of concerts, and

has heard nearly all the musical celebrities from Julian in 1854 down. He has never done any teaching, but was choir leader and organist in New York for many years. Mr. Main is a skillful, prolific, original, and versatile composer. His first tune was written in 1855, and since then he has written over a thousand pieces—all sorts—part songs, singing school pieces, Sunday-school songs, hymn tunes, gospel hymns, anthems, sheet music songs, love songs, quartets, and instrumental pieces.

The only instruction in harmony and musical composition he has ever had was one quarter's lessons with Prof. Geo. W. Pettit and another quarter's tuition with the venerable Thos. Hastings, Mus. Doc. All his other musical education he obtained by exercising his Yankee propensity for asking questions.

Among fifty or more pieces, which might be mentioned as his most popular ones, the following well-known songs may be named: "We Shall Meet Beyond the River," "The Bright Forever," "In the Fadeless Spring-time," "Clare—In Heavenly Love Abiding," "Blessed Homeland," "O How He Loves," and many others.

Mr. Main is a veritable antiquarian in old music books. This propensity asserted itself in 1861, when he dug out from a pile of rags in a tin-shop a copy of Daniel Read's "Columbian Harmonist, No. 1," 1793. His collection increased until 1891 he sold to the New-berry Library of Chicago over thirty-five hundred volumes, where they are known as the "Main Library." Among the number were over two hundred American books between 1721 and 1810. He still has a modest little library of some 4,000 volumes. He has musical autographs and manuscripts of many of the musical celebrities.

Mr. Main has a wonderful memory for names and dates. He knows the names of hundreds of tunes, their authors, with date of birth and death, and, in many cases, the date of the copyright. He is an authority in the matter of copyrights, and can tell in most cases instantly whether a song is copyrighted and who owns it, or knows where to look for the information. In this respect he is unique. There is not another individual in America, so far as we know, who knows as much about old church music, especially that of American origin, as he does. He can take a new hymn and tune book, and go through it and mark every well-known tune in it, and many of the less known American and foreign, as regards composer, owner, copyright, dates, etc., at a single sitting without reference to his library, so extended is his knowledge and so reliable his memory. His knowledge and skill in this direction render his services invaluable to the publishers who have been so fortunate as to secure them.

As to his tastes in literature, he prefers biography and travels; is fond of poetry of the tender and pathetic; has a keen sense of the humorous, and is especially fond of the comical; in fact he can write a pretty good comic verse himself, but is too modest to show it to the world.

In regard to his religious proclivities, he was brought up a Methodist, joined the church in 1854 before he came to New York; but he quaintly says that he is not outrageously pious, and could laugh at a funeral, even his own, if he saw anything comical, and he could just as easily shed tears at anything tender and pathetic.

He is full of sunshine and good humor. He is immensely entertaining in his conversation, and one of the best of companions. His letters to his friends are usually full of wit and humor. He remarks that he might be more dignified, but it would increase his doctor's bills.

Concerning his tastes in music, he believes heartily in music for the masses, and endeavors to write mostly that grade of music. He believes there is a use for, and much good done by, gospel hymns and much other music that is frequently called trashy. While he respects all great composers he is a confirmed Wagnerite, and thinks there is no music like that of this great master. Personally he is an out and out Wagnerite.

Mr. Main is old enough to quit work, but he hasn't time to stop—so he is "still at it."

J. R. SWENEY.

XXIII

John R. Sweney

NOT every one who can write music can write such as will sway the multitudes and satisfy the demands of great occasions. The subject of our sketch was one of the most successful of these. Mr. Sweney has made his impress on the religious world. His music is sung everywhere, and if he had one characteristic more than another it was that of great power.

John R. Sweney was born in West Chester, Pa., December 31, 1837. He gave marked indications of musical ability at an early age. While yet a boy he began to teach music in the public school and to lead music in the Sunday-school. This musical work determined his whole future life. His love for music and his success in it led him to choose it for a profession. While thus teaching and leading it was his custom to occasionally compose for his school.

At the age of nineteen he began the study of music in earnest under Professor Bauer, a celebrated German teacher. He took lessons on the violin and piano. About this time he was chosen leader of a choir, and was also in constant demand for children's concerts and entertainments, as well as the conductor of a glee club.

At the age of twenty-two he was called to teach at

Dover, Delaware, where he was successfully at work when the war broke out. He then took charge of the band of the Third Delaware Regiment, and continued till bands were disbanded by the government.

After returning from the war he was appointed Professor of Music at the Pennsylvania Military Academy, then located at West Chester, Pa. Previous to this time he had written several pieces for the piano, which were published. Three years after, the Pennsylvania Military Academy was removed to its present location, Chester, Pa., but at the solicitation of many friends he remained in West Chester, and put his energy into his teaching there, especially his band, until "Sweney's Cornet Band" became famous in that part of the state.

About 1869 he was recalled to the Pennsylvania Military Academy, and moved to Chester, where he was professor of music in that institution for twenty-five years.

In 1876 the academy conferred on him the degree of Bachelor of Music, and in 1886, the degree of Doctor of Music was conferred on him by the same institution.

In 1871, having connected himself with the church in Chester, he began the composition of sacred music, and soon became widely known, and was in great demand as leader of large congregations.

For many years he led the vast assemblies at the well-known summer meetings at Ocean Grove, N. J. He also had charge of the music at Lake Bluff, near Chicago; at New Albany, Ind.; Old Orchard, Me.; Round Lake, N. Y.; Thousand Islands, and many other places; in fact, he was one of the most popular and successful song leaders in the country. It was a common saying among evangelists that "Sweney knows how to make a congregation sing."

For ten years or more he had charge of the music at Bethany Presbyterian Church and Sunday-school in Philadelphia, of which school the Hon. John Wanamaker was superintendent—one of the largest Sunday-schools in the United States.

Mr. Sweney wrote over one thousand sacred songs. Among his most popular ones are: "In the Morning," "Light after Darkness," "Sunshine in the Soul," "More about Jesus," "Tell Me How," "Oh, 'tis Glory," "The New Song," "I Will Shout His Praise in Glory," etc., but the most popular and widely known, and the one that is sung in almost every language, is "Beulah Land."

His first Sunday-school book, the "Gems of Praise," was issued in annual numbers beginning in 1871 and finished in 1876. He was then associated largely with Mr. Wm. J. Kirkpatrick in issuing the following books: "The Garner," "The Quiver," "The Ark of Praise," "Songs of Redeeming Love—Nos. 1 and 2," "Joy to the World," "Wells of Salvation," "Gospel Chorus" (male voices), "Our Sabbath Home," "Melodious Sonnets," "Joyful Sound," "On Joyful Wing," "Precious Hymns," "Quartette," "Trio," "Temple Trio," "Revival Wave," "Infant Praises," "Emory Hymnal," "Showers of Blessing," "Temple Songs," "Prohibition Melodist," "Sunlit Songs," "Radiant Songs," "Songs of Triumph," "Glad Hallelujahs," "Songs of Joy and Gladness—Nos. 1 and 2," "Hymns of the Gospel—New and Old" (published in London, England), two anthem books called—"Anthems and Voluntaries" and "Banner Anthems," and in connection with the Hon. John Wanamaker, "Living Hymns." Mr. Sweney also wrote a number of services and cantatas, and associated with Mr. Kirkpatrick a temperance cantata entitled, "The Water Fairies." He also edited a number of other books.

Mr. Sweney was editor or associate editor of about sixty books. He spent a busy life and was very popular. He was the right man in the right place. "Blessed is the man who has found his work; let him ask no other blessedness." "Know thy work, and do it; and work at it like Hercules."

Mr. Sweney passed away peacefully in the presence of his wife and children, April 10, 1899.—A life well spent in the service of Sacred Song.

> " Mourn not the dead whose lives declare
> That they have nobly borne their part,
> For victory's golden crown they wear,
> Reserved for every faithful heart."

W. J. KIRKPATRICK.

XXIV

Wm. J. Kirkpatrick

THERE are but few gospel song composers who are better and more favorably known than the subject of this sketch, Wm. J. Kirkpatrick, born February 27, 1838. His father, Thompson Kirkpatrick, was a school teacher and music teacher, and well known as a musician in Mifflin, Juniata, Cumberland and Perry Counties, Pennsylvania.

William J. grew up in a musical atmosphere, and at an early age learned to play upon the fife, flute, violin, and later upon the violincello. In the spring of 1854 he left his home in Duncannon, Perry County, Pa., for Philadelphia to study music and learn a trade, and served over three years at carpentering. He was much more interested in music than in mechanics, devoting all his leisure time to its study. His ambition at this time was to become a violinist.

In February, 1855, he joined the Wharton Street Methodist Episcopal Church, of Philadelphia, and from that time devoted himself mostly to sacred music, giving his services to the choir and Sunday-school. As there were few organs in the churches in that early day, his violin and 'cello were in constant demand for choir rehearsals, singing societies and church entertainments. During this preliminary time he composed a number of hymn tunes and anthems, but they were not offered for publication.

He studied vocal music under Prof. T. Bishop, then a leading oratorio and ballad singer, and became a member of the Harmonia and the Handel and Haydn Sacred Music Societies, where he heard the greatest singers of the day and became familiar with the principal choral works of the great composers.

His first published composition, entitled, " When the Spark of Life is Waning," appeared about 1858, in the *Musical Pioneer*, of New York.

In 1858, at twenty years of age, his first editorial work was begun in this way : One Sunday afternoon at the close of the Sunday-school, somebody was singing a hymn to Mr. A. S. Jenks, Bible-class teacher and musical enthusiast, who had recently published a large collection of camp-meeting songs which was very popular. While the hymn was being sung, young Kirkpatrick wrote off the melody, harmonized it and gave it to Mr. Jenks, who seemed amazed at this exhibition of home talent. Mr. Jenks, who was then collecting material for a music edition of his popular book, took the music to his musical friends in New York, where he expected to have the work done. The arrangement stood the test of criticism, and Mr. Kirkpatrick was engaged to prepare the matter for the typographers, read the proofs, and get up the book.

Soon he was to be found in company with Mr. Jenks, taking down melodies at camp-meetings and elsewhere from many of the famous singers of that kind of music. He prepared the music for publication in " Devotional Melodies," a book issued by Mr. Jenks. This experience had much to do in giving direction to the development of Mr. Kirkpatrick's talents and prepare him to write the many popular sacred songs which appeared later.

For several years he devoted himself exclusively to the study, practice, and teaching of music, giving special attention to theory, harmony, and composition under the excellent instruction of Dr. Leopold Meignen, conductor of the Harmonia Society.

Mr. Kirkpatrick was married in 1861, and in December of the same year connected himself with the 91st Regiment P. V. (Col. E. M. Gregory) as principal musician (fife major). He remained with the regiment in that capacity, mostly in Washington and Alexandria, until October 9, 1862, when his position was abolished by general orders. He returned to Philadelphia, but went into other pursuits at that time more remunerative than music, but continued his work and interest in choir, Sunday-school, and singing-class work, being leader, organist, and Sunday-school chorister in several of the prominent Methodist and other churches of that city. In 1865 he was elected organist, and leader of all the music of the Ebenezer Methodist Episcopal Church, which position he held at three different periods for over seventeen years. He studied the pipe organ under the well-known blind teacher and organist of St. Steven's, Mr. David D. Wood. Vocal lessons were received from some of the great Italian teachers.

He was again engaged by Mr. A. S. Jenks to supervise the issue of a hymn and tune book, "Heart and Voice." The entire work of selecting, classifying, and arranging the twelve hundred hymns, with appropriate tunes, of this four hundred and forty-eight page book was committed to his care. On the completion of this book in 1866 he accepted a responsible position in a furniture manufactory, of Philadelphia, where he remained, with a short interruption, for ten years. During the latter part of this time, from 1872 to 1875, his first popular gospel songs, words and music were written and published. " Resting at the Cross," " Sweetly I'm Resting in Jesus," " Beautiful Day," " Companionship with Jesus," " Entire Consecration," " Wait and Murmur Not," etc.; also "Leaflet Gems, Nos. 1 and 2," were all issued in 1875. " Precious Songs " was published in conjunction with Rev. J. H. Stockton, whose beautiful and popular melodies Mr. Kirkpatrick had been arranging and harmonizing for several years before.

Mr. Kirkpatrick's songs were now in great demand, and several publishers procured a number of his compositions. About this time he became acquainted with Mr. John R. Sweney, of Chester, Pa., who was then making his mark in musical composition, and it was not long before a proposition was made and accepted to unite their efforts on a book.

Upon the death of his wife in May, 1878, and the dissolution of the co-partnership of the firm with which he had been engaged, a month later, he resolved to abandon the furniture business entirely, and, after an extensive tour through the country during June, July and August, he began in September, 1878, to devote his entire time to the composition and teaching of music—organ, piano and singing. In 1880 his first book as an associate of Mr. Sweney, the " Quiver of Sacred Song," was published by Mr. John J. Hood.

From 1880 to 1897 in connection with Professor Sweney, forty-nine books were issued by eight publishers in the United States, and one in London, England. This list includes six books especially prepared for Sunday-schools, and five anthem books for the choir, but does not include the many small books, nor annuals and services for Easter, Children's Day, Christmas, etc. All of these publications sold well, and the aggregate sales foot up into the millions.

From 1886 to December, 1897, Mr. Kirkpatrick had charge of all the music in Grace Methodist Episcopal Church, Philadelphia. He gave up teaching music in 1889, and devoted all of his time to composition, church and Sunday-school work, convention and camp-meeting singing, where he has taken great pleasure and interest in leading the people in sacred song, and obtaining the best possible results with the least amount of self-display.

Since the death of Mr. Sweney, Mr. Kirkpatrick has given up all of his public leading and singing, but has still been adding to his list of books. And since 1897 no less than forty-two have been issued, upon which appears his name as editor or associate editor, besides many smaller books, services, etc., which bear the imprint of over a score of publishers.

Among the best known of his recent books are: " Young People's Hymnal, Nos. 1, 2 & 3," " Sunday School Praises," " Jubilant Voices," " Devotional Songs," " Glorious Praise," " The Redeemer's Praise," " Joy and Praise," " Hymns and Spiritual Songs, No. 2," etc.

Mr. Kirkpatrick was married the second time, October, 23, 1893, to Mrs. Sara Kellogg Bourne, of New York. During 1905 they travelled together through France, Germany, Switzerland and England.

Mr. Kirkpatrick is president of the Praise Publishing Company, of Philadelphia. He is a busy man and always does his work in a scholarly manner.

He resides in Philadelphia, but spends several months each year in his winter home, " Sunny Croft," Winter Park, Florida.

REV. E. A. HOFFMAN.

XXV

Rev. Elisha A. Hoffman

THE subject of this sketch, Elisha A. Hoffman, was born in Orwigsburg, Schuylkill County, Pa., on the seventh day of May in the year of our Lord 1839. His parents, Francis A. and Rebecca A. Hoffman, were Pennsylvania Germans. His father was a minister of the Gospel in the Evangelical Association, and rendered over sixty years of service in preaching the word.

He was educated in the public schools of Philadelphia, the city of Brotherly Love, and graduated, in the scientific course, from the Central High School. Afterwards he took up the classics and completed a classical course in Union Seminary, of the Evangelical Association. For eleven years he was connected with the Association's publishing house in Cleveland, Ohio. His musical education was limited. He is no graduate from any School of Music, but the best of all he is a natural musician. All the musical knowledge he has was gained by personal application.

Mr. Hoffman's first impressions of music came from hearing the voice of sacred song in the home. His parents both had sweet voices and sang well. It was their custom, in the hour of family worship, both morning and evening, to sing one or two hymns. The children early became familiar with these hymns and learned to love them and to feel their hallowing and refining power. Their lives were marvellously influenced by this little service of song in the home. A taste for sacred music was created and developed, and song became as natural a function of the soul as breathing was a function of the body.

Under the power of such an environment, Mr. Hoffman came to consciousness of a princely possession with which God had endowed him—the ability to express his intuitions and conceptions in meter and song. His inner being thrilled with inspirations, longing for expression, and he used the power with which God had clothed him in the production of the many songs which bear his name. His first composition was given to the world when he was eighteen years of age. Since then heart and brain and pen have been very prolific in the birth of songs.

Over two thousand of his compositions are in print. He has assisted in the compilation and editing of fifty different song books, some of which have received marked favor and have been issued in large editions. All have accomplished a measure of good, and have proved a blessing to the world. Many separate compositions have been translated into the languages of different countries, and from these many countries have come letters expressing gratitude to the author for their helpfulness and inspiration.

In the larger number of his musical compositions Mr. Hoffman is the author of both the words and music. When a melody is born in his soul, appropriate words seem to be immediately associated with the melody ; or, when a conception in his mind crystallizes into a hymn, usually there is present the suggestion of a melody that will give adequate and fitting expression to the mental conception. There are exceptions, but this is the rule which governs him in his musical writings.

Among his most popular and useful songs are: "What a Wonderful Saviour," "Enough for Me," "Are You Washed in the Blood?" "No Other Friend Like Jesus," "I Must Tell Jesus," and many others.

Mr. Hoffman has been a minister of the Gospel for many years, and is at present the pastor of the First Presbyterian Church of Benton Harbor, Michigan, and has served this church in this relation for over thirteen years. While his ministry in the churches which he has served has been fruitful, his songs in the good which they have done have constituted a still larger ministry. Through his songs he preaches to many thousands who never hear his voice.

FRANK M. DAVIS.

XXVI

Frank M. Davis

NO doubt every reader of these lines has often sung "Lord, I care not for riches" (with a reservation in some cases, perhaps, but none the less with pleasure and spiritual exaltation). It is a popular song and the people will sing it regardless of what the critics may say.

He wrote many other songs that are as good and nearly as popular, for instance, "Lead Me, Saviour," "Sheltered in Thee," "Flash the Toplights," "In Whom I have Redemption," "All the Way," "As We've Sown so Shall We Reap," etc.

The song entitled, "Is My Name Written There?" was composed in the month of July, 1876, while the author was at Burr Oak, Mich. "Lead Me, Saviour" was written, both words and music, on deck of an incoming steamer that plies between Baltimore and Savannah. It was a lovely August day in 1880 and the steamer was making her way up the Chesapeake Bay bound for Baltimore. In all the numerous books in which the song is to be found, it stands just as written on the steamer, although it was not played or sung for many days afterwards.

Frank M. Davis was born January 23, 1839, on a farm near the town of Marcellus, Onondaga County, N. Y. He was the youngest in a family of ten children. The family was musical, although none but

Frank chose music for a profession. When a mere boy
he began composing tunes, and setting words to them,
although he had never studied the laws of harmony.
These were crude and imperfect compositions, of
course, but with a persistent study of new music and
a careful observation of the construction of tunes he
kept improving, and although his father had set his
mind on making a farmer of him, he finally acceded to
his son's wishes to the extent of buying him an instrument; not a grand piano, however, but a four octave
Prescott Melodeon. The little treasure was brought
into the house on March 4, 1857. If the boy could
have written his now famous song at that time it
would have exactly expressed his sentiments.

Up to this time he had attended the village singing
schools, and was quite proficient in vocal music, and
with the advent of his melodeon he began the study
of instrumental music. It was not long till the
melodeon was exchanged for a piano and his studies
took on a larger range with more earnestness. Mr.
Davis travelled extensively, principally in the Eastern
and Southern states. He lived at different times in
Marcellus, N. Y., Vicksburg, Miss., Baltimore, Md.,
Cincinnati, Ohio, Burr Oak, and Findley, Mich. Being of a retiring disposition, he did not seek to make himself known, and was extremely modest; yet the music
which he sent forth won for him a name and fame
which shows how earnestly and faithfully he devoted
himself to his chosen profession.

He taught vocal classes and had charge of choirs
in various places and sang solos with great acceptance.
He also did much instrumental teaching. His first
composition given to the public was a march printed

in the *Waverly Magazine*. His first book for Sunday-schools, " New Pearls of Song," was published in 1877. Since that time he had published nine other books for Sunday-schools and temperance workers, all of which were well received and found ready sale. " Notes of Praise," published by himself, has reached near the 100,000 mark. His songs and music can be found in nearly every music book published. He was also author of over one hundred pieces of vocal and instrumental compositions published in sheet form.

Besides being a good musician, Mr. Davis was an artist of more than ordinary ability, as was evinced by the many beautiful pictures in oil, water color, and crayon which adorned the homes of his many friends where he visited. He was always busy with pen or brush when he was not engaged in study. He was a man of sterling qualities whose heart was filled with charity and brotherly love for all humanity. His music breathes forth that joyous, buoyant and sympathetic spirit which was his, and which he ever tried to infuse into the souls of others.

Mr. Davis died very suddenly of heart failure August 1, 1896, at Chesterfield, Indiana, camp meeting, where he had gone with friends to spend a few weeks basking in the sunshine of true spirituality, in which sort of religion he had been a lifelong believer. Mr. Davis was never married. His cousin, Mr. M. A. Dexter, took his remains to Findley, Mich., for interment. The funeral was held at the home of Mr. Dexter, where Mr. Davis had made his home at various times, and where his last book, " Brightest Glory," was edited and prepared for the press, music from which was sung on the occasion of his funeral.

There are thousands upon thousands who have been cheered and blessed by his songs. Dead, yet will he speak through coming years in the beautiful melodies which he created.

E. R. LATTA.

XXVII

E. R. Latta

THE subject of this sketch, Eden Reeder Latta, was born March 24, 1839, near Ligonier, Noble County, Indiana. This is a beautiful section of country known as "The Haw Patch." This section was also the early home of the well-known writer and musician, the late W. A. Ogden. The two boys associated together and were always very intimate friends. In after years Professor Ogden purchased a great many hymns from Mr. Latta, and set them to music, some of which became quite popular. Of a number of Mr. Latta's hymns, Professor Ogden said: "They are the very cream of Sunday-school song."

In his early career as a hymn writer, he composed his "Whiter Than Snow" for Dr. H. S. Perkins, of Chicago, who wrote music to the words, and the song was published in his book, "The River of Life," by Oliver Ditson Company, of Boston. The piece sprang into immediate and immense popularity, and besides being copied into many works, it was translated into other languages, for the use of missionaries. Mr. Latta attributes the great popularity and the long life of the hymn to Dr. Perkins' excellent music which he wrote to the words, but he says, "the words inspired the music." It is the perfect wedding of both words and music, that gives lustre, beauty, and power to a

composition. These wonderful sermons in gospel song
are a power for good beyond expression.

He has written a number of hymns for Mr. E. S.
Lorenz, as well as for many other publishers and composers. The beautiful poem which Mr. Latta composed
entitled, " No More Good-Byes," and set to music by
Mr. J. H. Fillmore, is one of the most beautiful songs
of its class. All Christian people are travelling, and
hoping at last to reach that far-off home, where there
will be " No more good-byes."

A number of years ago he wrote nine hymns in one
day for Mr. James McGranahan, now deceased. He
was informed that his hymns would go into competition
with the efforts of the ablest hymn writers. Out of the
nine hymns, six were taken, at $2.50 each.

One of his hymns, entitled, " Wandering Away," was
published in the " Harvest Bells," by Rev. W. E. Penn,
the noted Baptist evangelist, now deceased. Of this
hymn Mr. Penn said, " I have seen over five hundred
people come forward for prayer while this hymn was
being sung."

Mr. Latta has written, in all, upwards of sixteen hundred songs and hymns. In connection with his song
and hymn writing, he has revised hundreds of compositions for others : and from as far away as Central
America.

Last summer while Mr. Latta was attending the
Presbyterian Chautauqua and Bible Conference, at
Winona Lake, Indiana, he was the recipient of many
kind attentions, largely on account of the good record
which a number of his hymns have made. It does us
all good to meet the composer of the hymns and songs
that we use so frequently in our devotions.

He has done a good work, and his hymns will live and speak consolation to weary souls, when the author shall have passed over the river to join his loved ones who have gone on before.

P. P. BLISS.

XXVIII

P. P. Bliss

PHILIP PAUL BLISS was born in Clearfield County, Pa., July 9, 1838. His father and mother were religious and musical, and the home influence was such as to make good and lasting impressions upon the boy. He early developed a passion for music, and would sit and listen with delight to his parents singing when but a child, and very early sang with them.

The first piano he ever saw was when he was about ten years of age. He was a large overgrown boy, and one day down in the village, as he was passing by a house, he heard the sweetest music of his life. The door stood open and he was irresistibly drawn towards the sweet sounds that came from within. He was barefoot, and entered unobserved and stood at the parlor door listening, entranced, as a young lady played upon the piano. As she ceased playing he exclaimed with an intense desire, "Oh, lady, play some more." She looked around surprised, and with no appreciation of the tender heart that had been so touched by her music, said, "Go out of here with your great feet," and he went away crushed, but with the memories of harmonies that seemed to him like heaven.

His youthful days were spent on a farm or in a lumber camp, with the schooling the country afforded. In 1850 he made a public profession of Christ. He was immersed by a minister of the Christian Church. He afterwards became a member of a Baptist church that was near the school he was attending at Elk Run, Pa. He was naturally very religious from boyhood.

In 1855 he spent the winter in a select school at East Troy, Pa. In 1856 he worked on a farm in the summer and taught school in the winter at Hartsville, N. Y. He was then but eighteen years of age, and his quickness of mind for learning, and his industry in the improvement of opportunities, are in a marked way indicated by the fact that he was fitted to become a teacher.

The following winter he received his first systematic instruction in music. The school was taught by Mr. J. G. Towner, father of D. B. Towner. The same winter he attended a musical convention at Rome, Pa. In the providence of God the convention was in charge of Wm. B. Bradbury. From the time of this meeting Mr. Bliss cherished a deep affection for Mr. Bradbury, and a reverence for the gifts God had bestowed upon him as a composer.

In 1858 Mr. Bliss taught in Rome Academy, Rome, Pa. He boarded in the family of O. F. Young. Here he met the one who was as dear to him as the apple of his eye in the person of Miss Lucy Young. They were married June 1, 1859.

In July and August of 1860 a Normal Academy of music was held in Geneseo, N. Y., by T. E. Perkins, T. J. Cook, Bassini, and others. Mr. Bliss attended, afterwards taking up music teaching as a profession. He also attended the same normal in 1861 and 1863. In these times his teaching was done in the winter months. He worked on the farm during the summer.

The instructors of Mr. Bliss at these normals all speak in the highest terms of his unusual intelligence and remarkable proficiency.

Dr. Root said that "some time in 1863 he received a letter from Mr. Bliss that interested them very much. It accompanied the manuscript of a song. Would we give the writer a flute for it, was the substance of the letter, expressed in a quaint and original way, and in beautiful handwriting. We were on the lookout for bright men, and we felt sure that here was one. The song needed some revising, but we took it and sent him the flute.

"Later we made arrangements with Mr. Bliss to come to Chicago. It was agreed that he would go as our representative to towns that would naturally be tributary to Chicago, and hold conventions and give concerts (his wife being his accompanist), and so turn people's attention to us for whatever they might want in the way of music. For this service we guaranteed him a certain annual sum. If his concerts and conventions did not reach that amount we were to make it up.

"Mr. Bliss was constantly composing, and I soon saw that there was a man who had a 'call' both as a poet and melodist. His songs have been a wonderful power for good."

For four years Mr. Bliss remained in the employ of Root & Cady, holding conventions and giving concerts in towns of the Northwest. He afterwards continued the same work four years more independently. It was in the summer of 1869 that he first met Mr. Moody. After that he frequently led the music in the great preacher's meetings.

Mr. C. M. Wyman, since deceased, was at this time

working with Mr. Bliss, writing songs. They both
being earnest Christian men, attended Mr. Moody's
meetings together. Mr. D. W. Whittle says that he
thinks Mr. Moody got his first impression of the power
of solo singing in gospel work from these two men.
The first associated work of Mr. Whittle and Mr. Bliss
was in a Sunday-school convention at Winnebago, Ill.
Mr. Whittle was invited to address the convention, and
was told to bring a singer with him. Mr. Moody was
consulted as to a singer, and the result was Mr. Bliss
was chosen. He made a fine impression on the convention.

He was then engaged to take charge of the music in
the First Congregational Church of Chicago. After
three years, he resigned to enter the field as singing
evangelist with Major Whittle.

Mr. Moody, who was at this time in Scotland (in the
winter of 1873–1874), wrote a number of letters to Mr.
Bliss, urging him to drop everything else and sing the
Gospel. He also wrote many letters to Major Whittle,
urging that they two should go together and hold
meetings. They finally concluded to try a meeting or
two, letting the results help them to decide. The first
meeting was held in Waukegan, Ill., March 24th–26th.
The meeting was a memorable one. Major Whittle
says concerning it: " We returned to Chicago praising
God; Bliss to find substitutes for his conventions, and
I to resign my business position."

At this time Mr. Bliss' reputation as a composer was
being recognized everywhere, and his income from his
business was good and growing. Both he and his wife
were looking forward to the time when they could
settle down at home and live in comfort with a good

income from his musical writings; but as we have said before, Mr. Bliss was naturally very religious, and he felt that this was a call from God. He made a complete surrender of all former ambitions, and Major Whittle says, "Up to the day of his death I never heard him express a regret that he made his surrender and gave himself to God for His work."

They began immediately their joint labors as evangelist and singer, holding meetings in various towns in Illinois, Wisconsin, Michigan, Pennsylvania, Kentucky, Tennessee, Minnesota, Missouri, Alabama, Georgia, etc.

In September, 1876, he and his wife made a visit to Mr. Moody at Northfield, Mass. Mr. and Mrs. Bliss greatly enjoyed their visit, although both would laughingly mention Mr. Moody's method of making the best use of his visitors that he could, as manifested in using them in eleven meetings in a week. Mrs. Bliss was his constant companion, and greatly assisted him in his work.

The fame of the evangelists spread till their services were asked for in England. Mr. Moody urged them to go and they decided to do so. Their plan was to hold a meeting in Chicago, and as soon as that meeting was through go to England. It was now nearly Christmas and Mr. Bliss went home to spend Christmas with his family at Rome, Pa. He was advertised to sing in Mr. Moody's Tabernacle the Sunday after Christmas. A telegram was sent him to that effect, and it was while *en route* to this appointment that the great disaster occurred in which he and Mrs. Bliss lost their lives. This was December 29, 1876. Their train broke through a bridge at Ashtabula, Ohio, that spanned a chasm sixty feet in depth, carrying into eternity almost all on board. The train caught fire and was consumed. The next morning when word reached Chicago, Major Whittle and others went to the scene of the disaster, and, in Mr. Whittle's words, "remained there three days, until all the wreck had been removed, searching first for their bodies, then for anything that could be identified as having been connected with them. We found nothing. . . . They have gone, as absolutely and completely gone, as if translated like Enoch." They left two sons.

Prof. F. W. Root, in speaking of Mr. Bliss, says: "If ever a man seemed fashioned by the Divine hand for special and exalted work, that man was P. P. Bliss. He had a splendid physique, a handsome face, and a dignified, striking presence. . . . He had not had opportunities for large intellectual culture, but his natural mental gifts were wonderful. His faculty for seizing upon the salient features of whatever came under his notice amounted to an unerring instinct. The one kernel of wheat in a bushel of chaff was the first thing he saw. Examine the work which really enlisted his whole soul, and you will see nothing but keen discernment, rare taste, and great verbal facility. His gospel hymns contain no pointless verses, awkward rhythms or forced rhymes, but, on the contrary, they glow with all that gives life to such composition. He also had a natural instinct for melody. Mr. Bliss' voice was always a marvel to me. He used occasionally to come to my room, requesting that I would look into his vocalization with a view to suggestions. At first a few suggestions were made, but latterly I could do nothing but admire. Beginning with D-flat below (F-clef), he would, without apparent effort, produce a series of clarion tones, in an ascending series, until having reached G space above (C-clef) with pure tone."

His publications were "The Charm" and "Sunshine," for Sunday-schools (he also contributed largely to "The Prize," for Sunday-schools); "The Song Tree," a collection of parlor and concert songs; "The Joy," for conventions; and "Gospel Songs," for gospel meetings. He and Mr. Sankey compiled "Gospel Hymns and Sacred Songs, Nos. 1 and 2." He was author also of a great many sheet songs.

Many of Mr. Bliss' gospel songs have been sung around the world, and are still immensely popular.

MAJOR D. W. WHITTLE.

XXIX

Major D. W. Whittle

THE subject of this sketch, D. W. Whittle, was born in Chicopee Falls, Mass., November 22, 1840. He was named for the statesman whom his father greatly admired—Daniel Webster. There were three other boys in the family and before the outbreak of the war they had all joined the crowds of young men who were leaving New England for the Western states and had settled in Chicago. Mr. Whittle went into the Wells Fargo Bank as cashier. He soon became interested in the Tabernacle Sunday-school, the largest in the city, and in the course of time became its superintendent.

It would be hard to say just when he experienced his first deep interest in religious things; born of a sweet and lovely Christian mother, he probably learned while still a child what God's love and grace in the heart may mean; but it was characteristic of him that he made a definite surrender at a definite time of his heart and life to God. At midnight one night when he was acting as night watchman in the bank, he says: " I went into the vault and in the dead silence of that quietest of places I gave my life to my Heavenly Father to use as He would." This act was also characteristic of him in the *way* it was done; quietly and alone he settled the question with God.

It was through his work in the Tabernacle Sunday-

185

school that he met the woman who was to become his
wife—Miss Abbie Hanson. She was also a New Eng-
lander by birth.

In 1861 he joined the 72d Illinois Infantry, enlist-
ing in Company B as second lieutenant, but it was not
until 1862 that the regiment was ordered South, and
on the night before he left, August 22d, he and Miss
Hanson were quietly married, only to part the next
day for over a year.

Mr. Whittle served throughout the remainder of the
war; he became Provost Marshal on Gen. O. O.
Howard's staff; was with Sherman on his march to the
sea and was wounded at Vicksburg. At the close of
the war he was breveted "Major" and the title was
never dissociated from his name.

It was when he was sent home wounded from Vicksburg, having been shot in his sword arm while leading
a charge in place of his wounded captain, that he
first met the man who was to so greatly influence
his life—Mr. D. L. Moody. The following is the incident in Major Whittle's own words : " A big meeting of
some kind was being held in the Tabernacle, and with
some help I was able to attend, although I was still
weak from loss of blood and with my arm in a sling.
I was called upon to speak and as I got slowly to my
feet, feeling shy and embarrassed and weak, a strong
voice called out—'Give him three cheers, boys,' and
they were given with a will, for every heart was burst-
ing with patriotism in those days and the sight of a
wounded soldier in a blue uniform stirred the blood.
And how that kindly thought and that ringing cheer
stirred *my* blood ; how grateful I was to them—and
the one who called out, ' Give him three cheers ' was

Dwight L. Moody, and that is what his friendship meant to me from that moment onward; stimulating, encouraging, appreciating in a twinkling the whole situation—the young soldier's embarrassment, his need of a friendly word of help; and he was even then the born leader—'Give him three cheers,' and they cheered."

After the Civil War Major Whittle went into the Elgin Watch Company, and it was largely due to the influence of D. L. Moody who was already in evangelistic work that he gave up his business and became an evangelist. He always had with him a gospel singer and the first one associated with him was Mr. P. P. Bliss whose tragic death in the terrible Ashtabula disaster ended a most happy relationship.

Major Whittle wrote his first hymn in 1875— "Christ is All." He gave it to Mr. Bliss to set to music and after his death the words were found among his papers and later set to music by Mr. James McGranahan who succeeded Mr. Bliss as Major Whittle's singing companion.

The greater number of his earlier hymns were set to music by Mr. McGranahan—"The Crowning Day," "Showers of Blessing," and "I Know Whom I Have Believed" were among these. They made several trips to Great Britain together as well as extensive trips in this country, and were very closely associated until about 1890 when Mr. McGranahan's health began to fail and Mr. Geo. C. Stebbins took his place. His exquisite music is known and loved by all those who know gospel hymns; one of his most beautiful songs was composed for Major Whittle's words "Beyond Our Sight."

Nearly all of the Major's words were written under the *nom de plume* "El Nathan"; to some of his later hymns he signed his own name and the music to most of these was written by his daughter, Mary Whittle Moody; "Moment by Moment," "Be Still Sad Heart," "Blessed Hope," and "Still Waiting," are among these.

In speaking of his hymns he once said, "I hope that I will never write a hymn that does not contain a message—there are too many hymns that are just a meaningless jingle of words; to do good a hymn must be founded on God's word and carry the message of God's love." He also felt that the dignity of a gospel hymn deserved the best he could give, not only in material but in construction, and no rules of metre or rhythm were disregarded; he admired greatly the old church hymns and considered them a standard for all hymn writers. He composed about two hundred hymns. Mr. Moody said, "I think Major Whittle has written some of the best hymns of this century."

The last words he wrote have never been set to music; they were composed and dictated a few weeks before his death, during a night made sleepless by intense pain. The musical chiming of a little clock by his bedside made him think of the Old Testament High Priest of whose approach one was warned by the bells on his feet. Below we give this beautiful poem.

> " Swift, with melodious feet,
>   The midnight hours pass by ;
>   As with each passing bell so sweet,
>   I think, 'My Lord draws nigh.'

" I see Heaven's open door,
   I hear God's gracious voice ;
   I see the blood-washed 'round the throne,
   And with them I rejoice.

" It may be that these sounds
   Are the golden bells so sweet
   Which tell me of the near approach
   Of the Heavenly High Priest's feet.

" Not every night is thus ;
   Some nights with pain are drear.
   Then I join my moan with creation's groan
   And the chimes I do not hear.

" But the Lord remains the same ;
   Faithful He must abide ;
   And on His word my soul I'll rest,
   For He is by my side.

" Some midnight, sleepless saints,
   Made quick by pain to hear,
   Shall join the glad and welcome cry,
   ' The Bridegroom draweth near.'

" Then I shall see His face,
   His beauteous image bear ;
   I'll know His love and wondrous grace,
   And in His glory share.

" So sing my soul in praise,
   As bells chime o'er and o'er,
   The coming of the Lord draws near,
   When time shall be no more."

Major D. W. Whittle died March 4, 1901, at Northfield, Mass.

" Blessed are the dead which die in the Lord."

JAMES McGRANAHAN.

XXX

James McGranahan

JAMES McGRANAHAN was born July 4, 1840, near Adamsville, Pa., his ancestry being mainly of Scotch-Irish descent. His father, George McGranahan, was a farmer, hence James spent his boyhood on the farm. His father sent him to singing school, and he soon became assistant by playing the bass viol. At the age of nineteen he organized his first singing class, and soon became one of the most popular teachers in his section of the state. He longed for the opportunity of further musical study, but how to get it was no ordinary proposition, for his father's notions of the value of a musical education were far from comforting to his rising ambition. With characteristic pluck, he finally gained his point and won his father's reluctant consent by not only earning all his expenses, but also employing a man in his place on the farm, while he pursued his musical studies. It is easily surmised that he improved well his opportunities. That his father later revised his notions about the value of a musical education was very evident when no one rejoiced more than he that his son was being so marvellously used of God in winning souls through the power of persuasive song.

He entered the Normal Music School founded at Geneseo, N. Y., by Wm. B. Bradbury, where he pursued his studies under T. E. Perkins, Carlo Bassini, and

other eminent teachers.   Mr. McGranahan attended
the sessions of 1861 and 1862.   Here, too, he learned
other lessons than those set down in the books, for here
he first met Miss Addie Vickery, who afterwards became his wife, who being a ready accompanist, became
a most efficient helper in his later institute, convention
and evangelistic work.

In 1862 he became associated with the late J. G.
Towner, and for two years they held conventions and
made concert tours in the states of Pennsylvania and
New York, giving great satisfaction in the work.   He
now continued his musical studies under Bassini, Webb,
O'Neil, and others, studying the art of teaching with
that prince of teachers, Dr. Geo. F. Root, the art of
conducting with Carl Zerrahn, harmony under J. C. D.
Parker, F. W. Root, and, later, Geo. A. Macfarren, of
London.

In 1875 he accepted the position as one of the managers of Dr. Root's Normal Musical Institute, in which
capacity he served as director and teacher for three
years, Dr. Root continuing as principal.

During this time he was winning an enviable reputation in his convention work, and by his glee, chorus
and class music, and Sabbath-school songs published
from time to time.   His equipment at this time for a
successful career as a music teacher and composer was
complete.   He had become a cultured musician, with a
wide and growing reputation, his solo work attracting
much attention.

From his earliest years his rare tenor voice had been
the wonder and delight of all who heard it, and now
from some of his most eminent teachers came the pro-
posal that he should enter upon a course of special

training for the operatic stage, in which career it was felt he would certainly achieve fame and fortune. It was a dazzling prospect; but, on the other hand, his intimate friend, P. P. Bliss, who had given his wondrous voice to the service of song for Christ, was urging him to do the same. Comparing his long course of study and training to a man whetting his scythe, he insisted that his friend should "stop whetting his scythe, and strike into the grain to reap for the Master." Mr. McGranahan, however, felt distrustful both of his adaptation to such work and of his call to enter upon it.

Only a week previous to the Ashtabula disaster, Mr. Bliss wrote a letter to Mr. McGranahan on this subject. Before sending it he read it to Major Whittle with whom he had been discussing the matter as to what evangelist they should select to associate with Mr. McGranahan should he consent to take up the work. On the morning after the disaster Major Whittle and Mr. McGranahan met for the first time at Ashtubula, both on the same errand of mercy—that of recovering, if possible, the bodies of their dear friends, Mr. and Mrs. Bliss. Upon meeting Mr. McGranahan, Major Whittle's first thought was: "Here stands the man that Mr. Bliss has chosen as his successor." They went back to Chicago together, talked over the matter and prayed over it. Mr. McGranahan finally decided to give up all his future life to the service of God in song.

If the operatic world lost a star, the Christian world gained one of its sweetest gospel singers, and the hand of God was manifest in it all.

With a consecration that was most thorough, Mr. and Mrs. MacGranahan entered their new field, and to their great joy found it most congenial. For eleven years he and Major D. W. Whittle were associated as true yoke fellows in evangelistic work in various parts of the United States, Great Britain, and Ireland. Two visits were made to Great Britain, the first in 1880, when they had great success in meetings in which the leading ministers of the kingdom coöperated, in London, Perth, Glasgow, Edinburgh, Aberdeen, Dundee, Belfast, and other places. The second visit was made in 1883, when they were associated with Messrs. Moody and Sankey.

Mr. McGranahan's music has a quality that is all its own. It is characterized by strength and vigor. Much that he has written will live in the permanent hymnology of the church. Such songs as " My Redeemer," " I Shall be Satisfied," " The Crowning Day," " Showers of Blessing," " O, How Love I Thy Law," and many others will voice the praise of future generations in their worship of God. Mr. Sankey once said, " I believe the most beautiful gospel song Mr. McGranahan ever wrote is 'Sometime We'll Understand.'"

Mr. McGranahan was pioneer in the use of the male choir in gospel song. When holding meetings at Worcester, Mass., a draught which had not been noticed laid aside for the time being all the female voices, and he found himself with a chorus of male voices only. Always resourceful, he quickly adapted the music to male voices and the meetings went on with great power. What was necessity at first became a most popular and effective agency in the gospel work. Soon was published " Gospel Male Choir, Nos. 1 and 2," and the male choir and quartet are recognized forces in the Church to-day.

The following is a list of his principal publications :
" The Choice," and " Harvest of Song," in connection
with C. C. Case ; " Gospel Choir," with Sankey ; " Gos-
pel Hymns, Nos. 3, 4, 5, and 6," with Sankey and
Stebbins ; " Songs of the Gospel," and " Male Chorus
Book " were issued in England.

It may be of interest to the reader to know that
" El Nathan," to whom so many of the words are
credited, is the *nom de plume* of Major Whittle.

In 1887 a break in Mr. McGranahan's health compelled him to give up active work in the evangelistic
field. It was then that he built his beautiful home
among his old friends at Kinsman, Ohio, and settled
down to devote himself, in his semi-retirement,
to the composition of music which would still make
him a sharer in the evangelistic work of the period.
Though his health demanded limited hours at his desk,
yet he was a prodigious toiler while he could work,
and a large number of his best hymns were written in
these days.

Personally Mr. Granahan was a most lovable man,
gentle, modest, unassuming, in short, a refined and cultured Christian gentleman. He was a prince of entertainers. He loved good fellowship, and without effort,
apparently, on his part, his guests would be treated to
the most delightful social feast.

Mr. James McGranahan died July 9, 1907. He went
home to meet the Saviour whom he loved so well, and
served so faithfully.

IRA D. SANKEY.

XXXI

Ira D. Sankey

IRA DAVID SANKEY was born in the village of Edinburg, Pa., August 28, 1840. He was of Scotch-Irish ancestry. After some years his father, the Hon. David Sankey, and his mother, removed to a farm where young Ira grew up assisting in the farm work. He received the usual school privileges of those days.

In 1857 the family removed to Newcastle, Pa. This afforded him the opportunity of attending high school. Soon after arriving in Newcastle he joined the M. E. Church. Here he began his first choir work. His voice soon began to attract attention, and crowds of people came into the Sunday-school to hear the singing.

In 1860 he responded to the call of President Lincoln for volunteers, and enlisted in the Twelfth Pennsylvania Regiment. While in the army he frequently led the singing in the religious services. When his term of service as a soldier expired, he returned home to assist his father as a collector of internal revenue.

In 1863 he married Miss Fanny V. Edwards, who was truly a blessing and helpmate to him throughout his entire life-work.

Mr. Sankey was in possession of a fine voice, which had been enriched by cultivation, and his services as a gospel singer were in great demand in both Pennsylvania and Ohio.

In 1870 he was a delegate to the Y. M. C. A. Convention at Indianapolis, Ind. Here he first met Mr. Moody. The singing had been rather poor, and Mr. Sankey was asked to lead. He began by singing the familiar hymn, "There is a fountain filled with blood." The congregation joined heartily in the song, which put new life into the meeting. At the close of the service, the singer was introduced to Mr. Moody. Mr. Sankey describes their meeting thus: "As I drew near Mr. Moody he stepped forward, and, taking me by the hand, looked at me in that keen, piercing fashion of his, as if reading my very soul. Then he said abruptly, 'Where are you from?' 'Pennsylvania,' I replied. 'Are you married?' 'I am.' 'How many children have you?' 'Two.' 'What is your business?' 'I am a government officer.' 'Well, you'll have to give it up!' I was too much astonished to make any reply, and he went on, as if the matter had already been decided: 'I have been looking for you for the last eight years. You'll have to come to Chicago and help me in my work.'"

In 1871, after a delay of several months, and much urging on Mr. Moody's part, he consented to spend a week with him in Chicago; and before the week was over he resigned his government position and joined forces with him for their life-work. Thus began the great work of Dwight L. Moody and Ira D. Sankey that made the names of Moody and Sankey household words the world over.

Mr. Moody's keen intellect foresaw the great future for the young singer. He did not sing himself; but he said: "I feel sure the great majority of people do like singing. It helps to build up an audience—even

if you do preach a dry sermon. If you have singing
that reaches the heart, it will fill the church every
time. There is more said in the Bible about praise
than prayer, and music and song have not only accompanied all Scripture revivals, but are essential in deep-
ening spiritual life. Singing does at least as much as
preaching to impress the word of God upon people's
minds. Ever since God first called me, the importance
of praise expressed in song has grown upon me."

In October, 1871, the great fire occurred in Chicago,
which compelled them to suspend their work for a
short time. In 1872 Mr. Sankey moved his family to
Chicago. The evangelists then accepted an invitation
to hold services at Springfield, Ill. Their efforts were
crowned with success.

In 1873 they sailed for England, where they held
many successful meetings. Mr. Sankey's solo singing
was very effective. "Jesus of Nazareth passeth by"
was the most popular at this time.

The expression, "singing the gospel," was first used
by the Rev. A. A. Rees of Sunderland, England, in
describing Mr. Sankey's soul-stirring hymns. Gospel
songs were something new in that country at that
time. In Scotland they only used the Psalms of David;
others were called "human hymns," but with Mr.
Sankey's tact and skill as a singer and evangelist, he
soon won the hearts of even the bonny Scotland people
to sing "human hymns," and in such a prayerful spirit
that scores were brought into the kingdom.

Mr. Sankey composed his first gospel song, entitled
"Yet There is Room," while in Edinburgh, Scotland.
Dr. Horatius Bonar, who attended the meetings, wrote
the words.

While holding meetings in London, many of the prominent people attended, among whom might be mentioned the Hon. Wm. E. Gladstone, Lord Kinnaird, Queen Victoria, the Princess of Wales, and others. They enjoyed Mr. Sankey's solos, especially "The Ninety and Nine." The evangelists remained in Great Britain for two years, and held meetings in many of the leading cities of England, Scotland and Ireland. They returned to America in 1875.

Their first meeting after their return was held at Northfield, Mass. Then followed meetings in Brooklyn, Philadelphia, New York, Chicago, Boston, St. Louis, and hundreds of other cities were visited, not only throughout the United States, but in Canada and Mexico, and great good was accomplished wherever they labored. During the years which followed the evangelists made several trips to Great Britain. The campaign of 1881–1884 was a memorable one.

Mr. Sankey had delightful experiences on his visit to the Holy Land in 1898. He travelled over the road that Jesus travelled on His way to Calvary to die for the sins of the world. He sang on the Tower of David while at Jerusalem. He visited many of the ancient cities, and other places of interest, and wherever he went, his fine baritone voice was heard singing the songs of salvation.

Mr. Sankey was not only a great singer and his own best accompanist, but he proved a prolific composer, his original work being of a character that instantly commended itself to religious audiences. Mr. Sankey was one of the authors of the famous "Gospel Hymns," and of various other hymnals.

Among his most popular songs are: "The Ninety

and Nine," "The Cross of Jesus," "Jesus of Nazareth,"
"Onward and Upward," "There'll Be No Dark Valley,"
"Call Them Now," "A Little While," "Room For
Thee," "A Shelter in the Time of Storm," "Tell It
Out," "When the Mists Have Rolled Away," "While
the Days Are Going By," "Hiding in Thee," etc.

The history of the famous "Ninety and Nine" is
most extraordinary. While in Scotland Mr. Sankey
found the poem in a newspaper, which he was reading
on a train. He clipped the poem from the paper and
put it in his pocket. That very week Mr. Moody
preached upon "The Prodigal Son." At the conclusion
of his discourse he asked Mr. Sankey to sing something appropriate with which to close the service. "I
had nothing suitable in mind," writes Mr. Sankey,
"but at that moment a voice seemed to say to me,
'Sing the hymn you found on the train!' I thought
it impossible, but I placed the little slip on the organ
in front of me, lifted my heart in prayer, and began to
sing. Note by note the tune was given, and it has not
been changed from that day to this."

Mr. Sankey was a noble man. Among his gifts he
presented a handsome new building to the Y. M. C. A.
at Newcastle, the town in which he spent his boyhood.

Mr. Sankey spent the last few years of his life in
blindness. He died at his residence at Brooklyn, N. Y.,
August 13, 1908.

> "Out of the shadow-land, into the sunshine,
> Cloudless, eternal, that fades not away."

GEO. C. STEBBINS

XXXII

George Coles Stebbins

THE subject of this sketch was born February 26, 1846, in Orleans County, N. Y., where he spent the first twenty-three years of his life on a farm. In 1869 he removed to Chicago, which marked the beginning of his musical career. He became the musical director of the First Baptist Church in 1870, which position he held till the autumn of 1874, when he resigned to take up his residence in Boston. During his residence in the former city he became acquainted with Dwight L. Moody and with Ira D. Sankey, the latter coming to Chicago in 1870. Also with P. P. Bliss and with Major D. W. Whittle, both of whom early joined the great evangelistic movement inaugurated by Mr. Moody.

Shortly after his removal to Boston, Mr. Stebbins became the musical director in the church of which the late Dr. A. J. Gordon was pastor, remaining there till January, 1876, when he became the musical director of Tremont Temple, the pastor of which at that time was the late Dr. Geo. C. Lorimer.

In the summer of that year he had occasion to spend a few days with Mr. Moody at his home in Northfield, Mass., and during his visit there Mr. Moody induced him to enter evangelistic work under his direction, which he did that autumn. Mr. Stebbins' first work in this connection was to organize the choir for the meet-

ings that Moody and Sankey were to hold in the great
building erected for them in Chicago, and which were
to continue through October, November and December. During the remainder of the season he
assisted other evangelists ; and in the summer following became one of the editors of " Gospel Hymns," and
subsequently of the series of hymn books used by Mr.
Moody during the remainder of his life. Also afterwards the sole editor of " Northfield Hymnal."

Mr. Stebbins married Miss Elma Miller before entering on his musical career, and when he began his
evangelistic work she became actively engaged with
him, assisting him most efficiently in his singing, besides
conducting meetings and giving Bible readings for
ladies.

During the nearly twenty-five years of his association
with Mr. Moody, he assisted him and Mr. Sankey in
their work both in this country and abroad, besides
working with other evangelists, among whom were Dr.
Geo. F. Pentecost and Major Whittle.

In the autumn of 1890 he, with his wife and son,
went with the former to India for a season of work
among the English speaking inhabitants of that country ;
and during their stay there Mr. and Mrs. Stebbins and
their son gave services of song in several of the principal
cities of the country. On their return home they gave
services of song also in Egypt and Palestine, and in
Naples, Rome, Florence, Paris, and London.

From the beginning of Mr. Moody's work in Northfield, over thirty years ago, Mr. Stebbins has been one
of the leaders of the singing at the summer conferences
there, and is the only one now living having official connection with the work that has been present at every

general conference. He is also the only surviving member of the original group of men Mr. Moody had associated with him in his evangelistic work ; who were, beside himself, Mr. Sankey, Major Whittle, P. P. Bliss, and James McGranahan.

Regarding Mr. Stebbins' work, aside from his occupying important positions in churches, and his leadership in the great movement with which he was connected for so many years, he was frequently engaged to lead the singing at international and state conventions of the Y. M. C. A., Sunday-school, Christian Endeavor, and other religious gatherings ; among which may be mentioned the two greatest of the Christion Endeavor conventions, one held in Madison Square Garden, New York City, at which there were thirty thousand delegates ; and one held in Boston when there were fifty thousand present. Also the great Ecumenical Missionary conference held in Carnegie . Hall, New York, and the fiftieth anniversary of the founding of the Young Men's Christian Association in this country, held in Boston.

During these years his voice was not only heard in leading others, but it was in constant demand in solo singing, and on many occasions in singing with Mr. Sankey and others.

Mr. Stebbins was well equipped in this department of his work, as well as in the others, as he studied the voice with some of the most celebrated teachers in this country ; but much as his voice was heard in different parts of the world, he will be remembered best by the music with which his name is associated ; for that, if God continues to use it in the future as in the past, will long survive him and the memory of his public ministry.

Among his hymns that are most widely known, and which, it would seem, are most likely to endure, may be mentioned : " Saviour, Breathe an Evening Blessing," " There is a Green Hill Far Away," " Saved by Grace," " In the Secret of His Presence," " Take Time to be Holy," " The Homeland," and " O, House of Many Mansions." Only heaven itself can reveal in the fullest measure the great amount of good that Mr. Stebbins' gospel songs have accomplished in the world.

J. R. MURRAY.

XXXIII

James R. Murray

JAMES RAMSEY MURRAY was born at Ballard Vale, Andover, Mass., March 17, 1841, died in Cincinnati, Ohio, March 10, 1905. He was the son of Walter and Christine Morrison Murray of Roxburgh, Scotland, who came to America in 1840. The lad's early education was received in the public school, and later he began a business career with the Tyer Rubber Company. The late Mr. Tyer always expressed a strong interest in the ability of this youth. Next we find James taking music lessons and his talent was so pronounced that his friends advised him to devote his life to the musical profession. The Musical Institute at North Reading, Mass., 1856–1859, with Lowell Mason,, G. F. Root, W. B. Bradbury and G. J. Webb, as teachers, laid the solid foundation which his powers required, and he made most excellent progress. All his teachers loved him, but the lifelong tie that bound him to Dr. Root was the strongest friendship.

In 1862, Mr. Murray enlisted as a musician in the Civil War. His first song, " Daisy Deane," which proved to be the most successful of his early songs, was composed in camp in Virginia in 1863. The words of this were by his comrade and cousin, Thos. F. Winthrop. This song is known all over the world, and the Salvation Army uses an arrangement of it as one of their war cry songs.

At the close of the war Mr. Murray returned home, and taught the piano in his home town and other towns, but soon gave up teaching to accept a position with Root & Cady, Chicago, Ill., as editor of *The Song Messenger*, and assistant in the writing and publishing department. He remained with that company until the great fire in 1871, when he returned to Andover, and resumed his work of teaching music.

In 1868 he married Miss Isabel Maria Taylor, whom he had known from childhood. This gifted and finely trained woman with her excellent judgment supplementing his own invariably in the issue of all his compositions, and with a sense of the beautiful greater than his joy in music, made for him a home that was an ideal environment for his work. His are the happy songs of love of home and kindred, and the hope and faith these inspired have lifted the hearts of the homeless for the long years the two worked as one. Mr. Murray continued his musical work in Andover for ten years. He taught music in the public schools, was leader of choir and choral society, and an active temperance worker of the right kind.

In 1881 he was called to Cincinnati, Ohio, by the John Church Company to edit *The Musical Visitor* and to take charge of the publishing department. His taste and skill were recognized wherever American music was known.

Among the most popular of his gospel song books are: "Pure Diamonds," "Royal Gems," "The Prize," and "Murray's Sacred Songs." The following will recall some of his best loved sacred songs: "At Last," "Calm on the Listening Ear of Night," "I Shall be Satisfied," "There Shall No Evil Befall Thee," "Thine,

O Lord, is the Greatness," "The Way was Mine," "How Beautiful Upon the Mountains" and "Angels from the Realms of Glory." His life and songs were helpful to many way-worn travellers.

The last great labor Mr. Murray was engaged on for the John Church Company at the time of his break-down and subsequent death was the seeing through the press five volumes of Wagner's music dramas, with full score, original German text and a smooth and excel-lent English translation.

> " Put out the lights ;
> He will not need them more.
> His work is done ; his feet have gained
> The fairer, purer shore."

C. C. CASE.

XXXIV

C. C. Case

CHARLES CLINTON CASE was born near Linesville, Crawford County, Pa., June 6, 1843.

When he was about four years old the family removed to Gustavus, Ohio, where Mr. Case still resides.

The father, for his day, was quite an expert in the use of the violin, and the grandfather, a major in the Revolutionary War, was a successful teacher of vocal music.

When the boy was eight or nine years old, a neighbor gave him a small violin which, from the point of view of the old-time fiddler, he mastered long before he could read music.

He had an intense longing to learn to sing, but his parents discouraged him, thinking he had no talent in that direction. He was not allowed to attend singing school until sixteen years old, and then did so without the consent of his parents, borrowing the money of a neighbor.

His first instructor in vocal music was Mr. C. A. Bentley, who was a successful teacher of the rudiments of music, as well as a convention conductor of prominence. Bradbury's "Jubilee" was the book used in this school, and, though Mr. Case could not read music at all at the beginning of the term, after twenty-four lessons he had the satisfaction of being elected as-

213

sistant chorister of a choir of twenty or thirty voices in his own town.

For three winters in succession he attended Mr. Bentley's singing school, which met once a week. He worked on his father's farm during the summer season.

When nineteen years of age he taught his first singing school, but had no thought at this time of following it for a life-work. Later he taught a number of classes, and met with success and encouragement, and then he made up his mind to spend his life in the "vineyard of song."

Mr. Case used the violin in teaching for several years. During the first two years of his teaching this was the only accompaniment.

In April, 1866, he was married to Miss Annie Williams. From this time on the violin took a second place. For twelve years Mrs. Case attended every school and convention her husband conducted as accompanist. For the first few years this meant a good many hundred miles riding every winter through mud and snow. Later the railroads were used, a larger territory covered, and ten and four days' conventions held.

In the summer of 1868 Mr. Case attended his first normal, studying under B. F. Baker, of Boston. For the next eleven years he attended different normals during the summer, teaching the rest of the year. At these normals he studied with Dr. Geo. F. Root, Carl Zerrahn, Dr. Wm. Mason, Carlo Bassini, Dr. H. R. Palmer, P. P. Bliss, Dr. L. O. Emerson, Geo. Jas. Webb, and others, Mrs. Case attending and studying with her husband.

Soon after he began teaching, the parents of Mr.

James McGranahan moved to the adjoining county, only two miles away from his home, and the two young men became acquainted and steadfast friends, attending the normal schools together, and later were associated as business managers and members of the faculty of Dr. Root's Normal Musical Institute. Much credit for the great success of these normals was due to the efficient work of Mr. Case.

Mr. Case's musical composition dates from his attendance at Baker's school, his first hymn tune being published in Mr. Baker's " Jubilant Voices."

In 1875, in connection with Mr. McGranahan, "The Choice " was published, and two years later, "The Harvest of Song." About this time occurred the death of the lamented Bliss, a warm, personal friend of both, and Mr. McGranahan from this time on gave more attention to gospel songs, taking Bliss' place as singer for the Evangelist Whittle.

Mr. Case continued his musical conventions, and in 1879, in connection with C. C. Williams, issued " The Prince of Song," and a little later "Church Anthems." On the death of Mr. Williams, in 1882, Mr. Case joined Dr. Root in editing two Sabbath school books, " Pure Delight " and "Wondrous Love," and the singing school books, "Our Song World," "Arena of Song," and "Songs of the Assembly." In the meantime Mr. Case issued "The Pyramid of Song" and "Case's Chorus Collection." In connection with Mr. J. R. Murray, "Uplifting Songs." He also issued "Choice Songs." Nearly all of his books have been published by The John Church Company, Cincinnati, Ohio.

Professor Case has conducted the music at Chautauquas and other assemblies in various parts of the country. He has conducted large chorus choirs in Boston, Chicago, Cleveland, Akron, and Detroit. For ten years he spent a part of each season as leader and soloist in Mr. Moody's meetings. He was with him in his last work at Kansas City. During all this time the musical convention has had a large share of his time and attention.

Professor Case has accomplished a great amount of good in his line of musical work. May health and strength be his for many more years.

J. H. TENNEY.

XXXV

J. H. Tenney

ONE of the most prolific and popular song-writers of our times is Mr. J. H. Tenney. His writing has been confined chiefly to the demands of Sunday-schools, churches, choirs, singing schools and choral societies, and among this class of musical people he has won for himself high rank. In addition to the many books he has edited, his name appears in almost every Sunday-school, church or anthem book that has been issued for the last thirty or forty years, and some of his gospel songs are sung by all the prominent evangelists in the field. We have said that he is a prolific writer. He began early and has had little to hinder his steady application, and every-thing to favor the prosecution of his work. His father was a choir leader and an enthusiastic music lover, and his mother was the leading soprano in her husband's choir, and it was no wonder that the son was humming tunes before he had learned to talk! Then, at the age of eight, he could read plain music at sight, having attended singing school, and it was not much later when his favorite pastime was composing tunes (melodies) to hymns that he found in " Watt's Select Hymns." He would also write out these melodies on his slate or pieces of paper.

John Harrison Tenney was born in Rowley, Essex County, Mass., November, 22, 1840. Being born just after the campaign of " Tippecanoe and Tyler too," he was given the name John Harrison, after the successful presidential hero. He was not the hearty, healthy lad that loved romping and the sterner sports natural to boyhood, but was of a delicate constitution, and his preference ran rather to mental than to physical exercise. At school he was a favorite with his teachers on account of his studiousness and proficiency, and perhaps the lack of mischievousness that is common to boys. He may not have been so popular with the boys, as he did not care so much for their rough-and-tumble sports, but he was a favorite with his mother, who, by the way, was a gifted mother in every sense of the word. Their companionship was sweet and constant, and she knew just how to sympathize with her tender, diffident boy, and encourage him in his efforts and ambitions. Like all successful men, he now more than ever appreciates his indebtedness to his mother.

His school education consisted of that received at the district schoolhouse during the winter months. In the summer he worked on the farm and in the shoe-shop, for his father was a shoemaker as well as a farmer. Perhaps this is one reason why Mr. Tenney puts so much soul in his compositions. His evenings at home were usually spent with singing books, practic-ing in reading notes or singing favorite songs, and in this way he learned by heart every tune and anthem in his father's books. He also got hold of " Burrowes' Primer," and from it learned something about harmony and began to compose melodies and harmonize them.

Along in these times he became a subscriber to *The Musical Pioneer*, a paper that interested him greatly. It was food for his hungry soul. He fairly devoured its contents from month to month. By carefully observing the music in it, he soon felt encouraged to try his fortune in contributing to it. He prepared a few pieces, and with a palpitating heart and trembling hand dropped the sealed and addressed package into the post-office to await developments. On receiving the next number of the paper his apprehensions were resolved favorably—his efforts had been well received. The editor said, among complimentary things in the correspondence column, "it will be worth while for you to study music." He afterwards sent many contributions to the *Pioneer*, most of which were published. In fact, in one number of the paper nearly all the music was from his pen, although some of it bore a *nom de plume*. He afterwards contributed freely to the *New York Musical Gazette*.

Mr. Tenney is a very modest man. In fact, it is hard to get him to say enough from which to weave a sketch. To give the reader an idea of how he looks at it, we quote from an interview in which we asked for some of the facts concerning his life: " I have never done anything worth the telling, and all these laudatory notices are offensive to me. But if you are to say anything about me, I desire that it should be true and fair." But the thousands who have received so much pleasure and benefit from his musical compositions will not agree with him that he has "never done anything worth telling." Those who have sung or listened to his gospel song, "Where Will You Spend Eternity ?" will vote that he has served his generation pretty well, to say nothing of the popular songs entitled, "Jesus is Passing this Way," "Ever Will I Pray," "Hallowed Hour of Prayer," "My Anchor is Holding," "Beyond the Swelling Flood," "Onward Christian Soldiers," and numerous others which have been sung all over the land and are being sung now with such delight. Our author estimates the value of his labors too modestly.

Mr. Tenney has edited or has been associate editor of over thirty books, besides contributing to hundreds, and in many instances contributing largely. His books have been issued by so many different publishing houses that it is difficult to get a full list. We will mention a number of his more important works. "The Anthem Offering," "The Singing School Banner," "The American Anthem Book," "The Crown of Praise," "Temperance Jewels," "Golden Sunbeams," "Songs of Joy," "Songs of Faith," "Spiritual Songs, Nos. 1 and 2," "Gems of Gospel Song," "The Beacon Light," "Shining Light," "Sharon's Dewy Rose," "Sweet Fields of Eden," "Sparkling and Bright," "American Male Choir," etc., etc. This latter is his favorite book, although he takes pride in his work in "The American Anthem Book."

Mr. Tenney is a Christian—a deacon in the Congregational Church at Linebrook, Mass. For many years he gave his services as organist and choir leader.

In 1888 he married Miss Alice Potter, and two daughters and a son bless their home.

He delights in farm life, and to spend the evenings in giving vent to his musical nature in musical compositions. We are sure our many readers will join us in assuring our friend that we feel very much his debtor for the pleasure his delightful music has afforded us.

A. S. KIEFFER.

XXXVI

Aldine S. Kieffer

ALDINE SILLIMAN KIEFFER was born near Miami, Saline County, Mo., August 1, 1840. His father and mother, John and Mary Kieffer, emigrated to Missouri from Virginia in 1836. While his father was a farmer, he also taught singing classes. So Aldine's childhood was spent on a farm, and his first singing lessons were received from his father in the old schoolhouse on the prairie.

In 1847 Aldine's father died ; thus ended the singing class. However, his mother, having large faith in the possibilities of her boy to become a musician, gave him lessons. In 1848 his mother removed to Mountain Valley, now Singers Glen, Va. Here Aldine had the opportunity of studying music with his grandfather, Joseph Funk, a music teacher and publisher. His great love for music and poetry made the printing-office a kind of paradise to him.

He never had the advantages of literary schools, but the printing-office served as a good substitute in his case. The lad worked faithfully in the office, and Saturdays would attend the singing schools taught by Mr. Funk. Frequently he would walk five or six miles to attend these classes. In 1850 the printing-office of Joseph Funk & Sons began to assume larger proportions, both in size and business. Their book, " Genuine Church Music," having been revised, was now called

"Harmonia Sacra," and the notation changed from four to seven syllables.

At the age of sixteen Mr. Kieffer began teaching singing schools under the direction of Mr. Joseph Funk. The "Harmonia Sacra" was the book used. Mr. Kieffer continued to teach classes, and he gave every energy of his heart and soul to the cause of sacred music and poetry. He was wonderfully gifted as a poet.

In 1861, when the Civil War broke out, Mr. Kieffer suspended his singing classes, and entered the ranks of the Tenth Virginia Infantry, which was later attached to the Stonewall Division. He was in many hot engagements, and in 1864 was made a prisoner of war, and sent to Fort Delaware. Here he managed to get hold of a few music books, and spent his time in study.

When the war was over Mr. Kieffer returned home, and soon resumed his singing school work. In one of his classes he met a lady in the person of Miss Josie Hammon, daughter of Mr. Jacob Hammon, whom he married November 16, 1865. Mr. Kieffer then began his work afresh in the printing-office, and in 1867 he assisted in issuing the "Christian Harp," a small book for Sunday-schools, camp-meetings, etc., of which 128,000 copies were sold.

In 1868 he held his first normal music school; and in 1869 issued "The Song Crowned King," and in the same year composed his popular song "O, the Old Schoolhouse that Stands Upon the Hill." In 1870 the initial number of the *Musical Million* made its appearance, a journal of music, poetry, chaste literature, and the great advocate of character notes. Aldine S. Kieffer was its editor. This afforded Mr. Kieffer the opportunity of developing his powers in literature, poetry, music, and for the noble cause which he had espoused from boyhood, namely: the use of character notes ;—of this he was a strong advocate, and was eminently successful.

Mr. Kieffer held normal music schools in several different states. He organized the Virginia Normal Music School at New Market, Va., of which Prof. B. C. Unseld was principal. Annual sessions were held for several years.

The publishing business finally merged into the firm name, The Ruebush Kieffer Company, and in 1878 removed from Singers Glen to Dayton, Va. For years Mr. Kieffer was the only member of the firm who did any editorial work, either musical or in a literary capacity. He became famous in his line of work, and was in touch with many well-known musicians, among whom were: Theo. F. Seward, H. P. Main, J. R. Murray, W. T. Giffe, and scores of others. And in book association, J. H. Tenney, B. C. Unseld, W. B. Blake, J. H. Hall, and others.

Of the fifteen or twenty song books which he edited " The Temple Star " was the most popular. Over 500,000 copies have been sold.

Some of his most popular songs are : " The City of Light," " Olden Memories," " Home to My Mother in Heaven," " Grave on the Green Hillside," etc.

His book of poems, entitled " Hours of Fancy or Vigil and Vision," is highly worthy of a place in any library.

Professor Kieffer was a man of many excellent qualities, kind, sympathetic, and pleasant in his associations.

Prof. Aldine S. Kieffer died November 30, 1904, at his home in Dayton, Va. In the Dayton cemetery he sleeps in a " grave on the green hillside."

J. H. KURZENKNABE.

XXXVII

J. H. Kurzenknabe

THE subject of this sketch, J. H. Kurzenknabe, was born in Moenchehof, Kurhessen, Germany, June 18, 1840. He was left an orphan in childhood, and spent part of his early years in Cassel attending the public and industrial schools. On September 13, 1854, when emigration fever in that city was at its height, he secured the necessary papers, and with $400 in gold started for the promised land, America.

The long voyage in a sailing vessel via Bremen to New York lasted seven weeks, forty-nine days of storm and sunshine. Being already at his early age, fourteen years old, a clever violinist, he made friends on board by his frank manners and sweet music so obligingly rendered. An incident occurred here which in after time came back to bless and assist him:—Among the passengers was an aged lady whose children had preceded her to America, and then later sent for the old mother. She suffered from seasickness and weakness almost the entire voyage. The German lad, mindful of the loving kindness of a mother, of whom he was so early bereft, ministered to her wants, and paid her every attention until they landed in New York. Her children, who were there to meet her, soon learned of the kindness of the boy. " Save the boy;—the boy who was so good to your mother." In the family he found a temporary home and friends, and in after years was not forgotten.

J. H. Kurzenknabe is a born musician and followed the bent of his mind; later he went to school in a Pennsylvania seminary, where he attained an English education, and prosecuted his musical studies to make for himself a name as a teacher of vocal music, and of the violin. Still later he studied under Wm. B. Bradbury, one of America's greatest musical writers, and one of the noblest of men. Then he associated himself with that prince of musicians, Geo. F. Root, for a short time, and after that travelled through the states of New England, New York, New Jersey, Pennsylvania, Maryland, Virginia, West Virginia, and back again to Maryland, teaching classes, choirs, conventions, cornet bands, orchestras, and leading the music of teachers' institutes. He settled for a time, with headquarters at Hagerstown, Md., where at the age of nineteen to twenty he married a sweet-faced girl bride of fourteen and a half years, who brought sunshine to his life. He resided successively in Baltimore, York, Pa., Philadelphia, Camden and Moorestown, N. J., New York, Boston, Dedham, Mass.; then the Civil War came on and he went back again to Hagerstown. Then Sunbury, Mercersburg, McConnellsburg, Mechanicsburg, and at last Harrisburg, Pa., claimed him as a citizen, and would not permit him to get away. Here for the past forty years has been his home, where he has been engaged in writing songs, teaching music in almost every town and city in Pennsylvania and Maryland, and together with his sons has charge of a piano and music store.

Professor Kurzenknabe is highly esteemed in his home city for his generous disposition, his unbounded en-

thusiasm and social qualities. He has always been an
untiring worker, active in measures for the best interests
of Harrisburg. He was chairman of the Publication
Committee of the Board of Trade for the first twelve
years of its existence, and is honored wherever he is
known.

In 1894 the professor was the president of the
Pennsylvania State Music Teachers' Association, including in its membership all of the foremost teachers
and musicians in Philadelphia, Pittsburgh, and the leading cities and towns throughout the state.

J. H. Kurzenknabe's Sunday-school, day school and
church music books of which he has been the author
and publisher are known wherever song is loved. All
of them attained a large sale; one of them, " Sowing
and Reaping," sold over 300,000 copies, and all have
yet a fair demand.

Orders for his books, " The Reward," " Song Treasury," " Peerless Praise," " Gates Ajar," " Songs and
Glees," " Music at Sight," " Wreath of Gems," " Rudiments of Music," " Songs and Hymns," " Sowing and
Reaping," " Fair as the Morning," " Gospel Trio," " Kindly
Light," and " Sweet Silvery Echoes," have come from
almost every state and territory in the United States
and Canada, and books have been shipped to England,
Germany, Porto Rico, Australia, New Zealand, China
and Japan, and some of his songs have been translated
into German, Spanish, Hungarian, Swedish, Chinese
and Japanese.

St. John's Reformed Church, Harrisburg, Pa., where
he worships, he organized as a Sunday-school in 1893,
and in 1899 as a congregation ; there his remarkable
activity and faithfulness find their reward in advancing

years, happy to enjoy the fruit of his labors through grace of the Lord Jesus, which has sustained him in all his pilgrimage with richest mercies.

In 1904 Professor Kurzenknabe, accompanied by one of his daughters, paid a visit to the home of his childhood, and remained for three months in the Fatherland. Happy days were these, never to be forgotten. He kept a diary of his ten days' sea-voyage to Bremen, and to Cassel, to Frankfurt and Weisbaden. Thence down the German Rhine, the charmed river, to Mayence, Bingen, Ruedesheim, Saint Goar, Coblenz, Alternach, Remagen, Bonn, and on to Coeln (Cologne), eight days on the beautiful Rhine. Thence through Westphalia, the once kingdom of Jerome Bonaparte, back to Cassel and the many cities to Erfurt, Meiningen, Eisenach, to the Wartburg, and back to Cassel, and the scenes of his childhood days, thence to Berlin, Hanover, Bremen, and return passage to New York. Notes are gathered for a splendid lecture with which to delight his audiences wherever it is delivered by the professor.

In 1906 he met with the first serious illness of his life. Out gathering offerings for his beloved St. John's chapel then building, he received a stroke of paralysis, ascribed by his attending physician as due to over-enthusiasm, since which time his weakened health debarred him from following his loved profession of teaching; however to-day his body, every member, is again restored to its normal state, enabling him to meet lecture engagements, etc.

Professor Kurzenknabe is the author of a number of fine essays on topics very popular wherever delivered before a music-loving audience. " Music for the Masses " (a forcible plea for music to be taught in the

public schools), "Church Music," "Musical Culture,"
"An Evening with Song," "Music in the Sunday-
School," "Lost Opportunities," and the above described
German lecture, entitled "An Evening Abroad."

Professor Kurzenknabe has several important works
in manuscript ready for publication.

Professor Kurzenknabe and his charming wife are
cheered by their eleven surviving children, all musicians :
three sons, prominent musical writers, three other sons,
overseeing the music business, with two daughters assisting, and three other daughters, well settled in life. His
declining years are serene and happy. The Golden
Wedding of their honored parents on November 13, 1909,
surely will linger in their memory.

Two daughters and two sons have fallen asleep.
"What a gathering that will be" when, reunited, all
join in praising "Him who is worthy to receive power,
and riches, and wisdom, and strength, and honor, and
glory, and blessing, forever and ever."—Amen.

W. A. OGDEN.

XXXVIII

W. A. Ogden

WILLIAM AUGUSTINE OGDEN was born in Franklin County, Ohio, October 10, 1841. At the age of six years he moved with his parents to Indiana, where his early education was obtained in the district schools. He began the study of music in the singing schools of the community at the age of eight, and at ten could read church music fairly well at sight. A little later he could write a melody by hearing it sung or played. When he was eighteen years of age he began as chorister in his home church. The young man was a close student in both his music and literary work.

At the outbreak of the Civil War Mr. Ogden exchanged the soft and alluring music of peace for that of the martial notes of war. He enlisted in the Thirtieth Indiana Volunteer Infantry. He served in a number of the historic battles of the war. During the war he organized a male choir, which became pretty well known throughout the Army of the Cumberland.

After the war Mr. Ogden returned to his home in Indiana, and resumed his musical studies under some of the greatest musicians of that day. Among his teachers were Dr. Lowell Mason, Dr. Thomas Hastings, E. E. Bailey and B. F. Baker, president of the old Boston Music School. With Professor Baker he studied voice, counterpoint, fugue and higher harmony. Professor

Baker was one of the most prominent teachers of his time, and Mr. Ogden made good use of the time he spent under him, and held him in grateful remembrance for the fine instruction received. He soon developed a great talent as a composer of music, and in 1870 issued his first song book, " Silver Song," which became immensely popular. This book was also published in England, and reached the enormous sale of 500,000 copies.

Professor Ogden also won distinction as a teacher and convention conductor. He taught in many of the states of the Union, and also in Canada. At the close of a normal, of which he was principal, at Greensburg, Pa., he was presented with a gold watch, which he prized very highly. For six years Professor Ogden held the position of director of music at the Iowa Normal School.

In 1881 he moved with his family to Toledo, Ohio, where he did the greatest musical work of his life. In 1887 he was appointed superintendent of music in the public schools of Toledo, which position he held until the time of his death. He enjoyed teaching the children more than any other work. Professor Ogden was very popular with the children, and his training of three thousand children in 1894 was the distinct triumph of the great Saengerfest, held in his home city.

Professor Ogden was a prolific composer of both words and music, and his writing was always characterized with beautiful thoughts. He was an educated musician and possessed most excellent taste, so that all his compositions are models of beauty and correctness. As a writer of Sunday-school and anthem music he excelled. He was particularly happy in his melodies, and this, with the fact that his harmony was pleasing, accounts for the immediate popularity which his music always attained. He was a musical genius, and his love and devotion to his art won for him distinction among musicians.

Among his many publications we mention the following: "Crown of Life," "Way of Life," "Joy Bells," "Notes of Victory"; in connection with Mr. E. S. Lorenz, "Gathered Jewels, Nos. 1 and 2"; associated with Mr. W. T. Giffe, "Spirit of Song" and "Happy Day," and "Best Endeavor," with Mr. Chas. Edw. Prior as associate. He also issued "Anthem Choir," "Royal Anthems" and "Bright Anthems," "Silver Carols," "Song Leader," "Drill Master," "Song Chief," "Convention Choruses"; the oratorio, "Josiah," and the oratorio "Birth of Christ." He was also author of two cantatas, and two comic operas.

Professor Ogden composed scores of popular and exceedingly useful gospel songs, a few of which are: "Gathering Home," "Where He Leads I'll Follow," "Seeking the Lost," "What Shall It Profit Thee?" "Look and Live," "Bring Them In," "Go and Inquire," "Toiling for Jesus," and many others.

Professor Ogden was a very genial and companionable man, and had the highest regard for the rights of other people; in short, he was a Christian and citizen of honor. He was very enthusiastic in his work, yet very gentlemanly and considerate.

Prof. W. A. Ogden died October 14, 1897. The funeral was said to be one of the largest ever seen in Toledo. He is gone, but his music and musical work will live and go on doing good. Though the singer be forgotten his songs will not die.

B. C. UNSELD.

XXXIX

B. C. Unseld

THE subject of this sketch, Benjamin Carl Unseld, was born October 18, 1843, at Shepherdstown, W. Va. After leaving school at about the age of fourteen, his youthful years, until he was twenty-three, were spent in commercial pursuits, progressing from clerking in a country store to the general offices of a railroad in charge of the general ticket department.

His first musical instruction was received when he was about fifteen years old from a companion who had attended a singing school. He was shown the representation of the scale in the old " Carmina Sacra," and had it sung for him ; but he doesn't remember how he learned to read music. He had a sweet boy's voice and a correct ear, learning any song by rote very readily. At the suggestion of the same musical companion, he obtained permission from his pastor to practice on the church organ.

Both boys being employed during the day, their only opportunity for practice was after the stores closed at nine o'clock at night, and an occasional hour at noontimes. They went to the church together and took turns, one at the keyboard and the other at the bellows. It was something of a strain on the courage of a couple of timid boys to go into a big empty, gloomy church gallery at night with only a dim lantern

—and war times at that ! In order to get more practice, young Unseld made a diagram of the keyboard upon " pasteboard," and practiced at home, picking out tunes from the " Carmina Sacra," so that when he went to the organ he was somewhat familiar with the position of the tune on the keyboard.

Shortly after the great battle at Antietam, a part of which he witnessed, September 17, 1862, he left home and obtained a position as bookkeeper in the general offices of a railroad at Columbia, Pa. Although engaged in business affairs he had some opportunity for musical improvement. He sang in a choir, and thus obtained practice in reading music and familiarity with high class compositions; he rented a melodeon and spent much time in his room improvising upon it; he bought a copy of " Woodbury's Harmony and Musical Composition," and studied it as well as he could without a teacher. This was his first real study of music. He accepted an invitation to play the cabinet organ in the Methodist Church on condition that the tunes should be given him early in the week so he could learn them. This was his first position as organist.

The desire for musical improvement becoming stronger and stronger, he decided to take a vacation from business for six months and study music—learn all about it in fact ! In the spring of 1866 he entered the Musical Institute at Providence, R. I., conducted by Eben Tourjee, afterwards Dr. Tourjee, the founder of the New England Conservatory at Boston.

Here he took up the study of voice, piano, organ and harmony. Dr. Tourjee, learning that the young man had had office experience, made him secretary of the school and in 1867, when Dr. Tourjee and Robert

Goldbeck established the New England Conservatory,
Mr. Unseld was with them and became the first secre-
tary of that widely known institution. While in
Boston, besides Dr. Tourjee and Dr. Goldbeck, Mr.
Unseld had the good fortune to number among his
friends such men as Carl Zerrahn, L. H. Southard,
G. E. Whiting, Luther W. Mason, Lewis Monroe,
H. E. Holt, and others of like prominence. To know
these men, meet them and converse with them almost
daily, was in itself an education.

In the summer of 1870 he attended a normal music
school conducted by Theo. F. Seward, with whom was
then begun an attachment that continued until Mr.
Seward's death. Here he also first met the veteran
voice teacher, Geo. J. Webb, and the great pianist and
teacher, Dr. Wm. Mason. Mr. Unseld is one of the few
living teachers who had the high honor of a personal
acquaintance with the great father of American music,
Dr. Lowell Mason, whom he first met that summer.
He enjoyed the rare privilege of visiting him in his
home.

In 1871, 1872, and 1873 he attended the school conducted by Mr. Seward, and officiated as the secretary.
At these sessions he formed acquaintances with some
who afterwards became famous in the world of music
—C. G. Allen, J. A. Butterfield, W. S. B. Mathews,
W. H. Sherwood, James McGranahan, C. C. Case, and
others of like renown. From 1871 to 1880 he was engaged principally in institute and general class work.
In 1874 he taught in Fisk University, Nashville, Tenn.,
and assisted in training the celebrated Jubilee Singers
for their European trip. In 1877 and 1878 he was
organist and choir master at St. James' Episcopal

Church, Lancaster, Pa. In 1879 he took up his headquarters in New York City, and for fifteen years was busy with class teaching, choir leading, public school music, summer normals, etc., besides composing, compiling, and editing numerous musical publications, including, in association with Theo. F. Seward, the extensively circulated tonic sol-fa works. His musical headquarters in New York was at the great publishing house of The Biglow & Main Co. Here he was in almost daily association with popular composers and teachers—Ira D. Sankey, Dr. H. R. Palmer, Hubert P. Main, Dr. Robert Lowry, and others of renown.

In 1894 he took up his residence in Cincinnati, Ohio, and was connected in an editorial capacity with the Fillmore Music House, with which company he still remains in affiliation. In 1898 he removed to Dayton, Ohio, and was employed in a similar capacity with the Lorenz Publishing Company. In 1901 he resumed his residence in New York, where he remained until 1905, when he removed to Hagerstown, Md., where he at present (1911) resides.

In 1874 the Virginia Normal Music School was founded at New Market, Va., through the efforts of Aldine S. Kieffer, with B. C. Unseld as the principal. This was the first real normal held in the South (since the Everetts' time), and is the mother-school of the whole system of similar schools which became so popular all over the South. Many of the most successful teachers and composers of the South were its pupils or pupils of its pupils. As the principal of that school it can be justly claimed for Professor Unseld that he is the musical father or grandfather of nearly all the successful normal teachers of the South. Professor Unseld is a persistent student of methods of teaching, and is peculiarly well prepared as a normal teacher. His teaching is in some respects better than that of any other normal teacher, in that he does not confine himself to the method of any one man or system. He selects the best points of all methods, and gives his pupils that which will be most useful to them in their work.

Professor Unseld is blessed with a genial disposition, a cordial manner, an attractive presence, winning at once the good will of pupils and the lasting friendship of all. He was married in 1887 to Miss Sally H. Rickard, of Shepherdstown, W. Va. Mrs. Unseld is an accomplished musician, having made music a special study in her school days and winning gold medals for proficiency. She plays the piano and organ and has a pleasing contralto voice, is a fluent and accurate sight-reader, both vocal and instrumental, and has the rare gift of absolute pitch, being able to name the key of any piece she hears or any succession of chords as they are struck on the piano.

As a composer of vocal music and compiler and editor of music books, Mr. Unseld has a wide reputation. He is the author, alone or in association with others, of over a score of music books, some of which have attained a sale of over a million copies. He was an editor of a number of important works of wide circulation in which his name does not appear in that capacity, including two in tonic sol-fa notation and negro dialects for use in Africa. His most popular song, " Twilight is Stealing," has been sung by millions of singers during the last twenty-five years and is still in demand.

A vote of thanks is due Prof. B. C. Unseld from

nearly the whole teaching and gospel song writing fraternity of the South for the noble service which he has rendered in making this musical progress possible.

Some day when our toils are o'er, we hope to meet and sing the " new song " in that beautiful home:

> " Far away beyond the starlit skies,
>   Where the love light never, never dies."

J. H. ROSECRANS.

XL

J. H. Rosecrans

THE subject of this sketch, James Holmes Rose-crans, was born at Berne, Albany County, N. Y., August 3, 1844. His father, who was a physician, died when the son was a lad of but eight summers. This necessitated James to make his own way in the world. He worked for several years on a farm, and being a lover of music, would spend his spare time in the study and practice of the "divine art." He also worked for some time in a flouring mill; but finally gave all up for music study. He entered Baxter's University of Music, Friendship, N. Y., which was then a very flourishing school. Prof. A. N. Johnson was president and Prof. James Baxter principal.

He was twenty years of age when he entered this school, and continued with it nearly four years, going into the country during vacation and at other times in order to get means to carry him through.

By the time he had studied two years in the music school he began to compose, and before he left it had published what proved to be a popular little cantata for Sunday-schools, entitled "Three Christian Graces." Some ten years afterwards he revised and enlarged it and called it "Faith, Hope and Love."

He also issued about this time a Sunday-school book which he called "The Little Sower." This book had a good sale, and some of his songs that are used to this day first appeared in it.

After a short itinerant life as a " singing teacher " he accepted a position in the Music Conservatory of Des Moines, Iowa. During this time he published a Sunday-school book entitled, " Pearly Gates." This book had a wide circulation.

About this time Mr. Rosecrans became acquainted with Fillmore Brothers, and contributed some very valuable songs to their first book, " Songs of Glory." This acquaintance soon ripened into a fast friendship, and ever since The Fillmore Brothers, of Cincinnati, Ohio, have published all of his musical works. For a number of years Mr. Rosecrans made his home with the Fillmores, at which time they worked together agreeably and profitably.

For several years he travelled among the churches teaching congregational singing and drilling Sunday-schools. From his lecturing he naturally became a preacher, and was ordained to the ministry of the Christian Church. He was called to be State Sunday-school Evangelist of California, in 1884, which call he accepted. He was quite successful, and has received similar calls to other states since, but has given his later years to the state of Texas. At present he is pro-·fessor of moral and mental science and Biblical litera-ture in Carlton College, Bonham, Texas.

Mr. Rosecrans is a fine Christian gentleman. Modest, unassuming, genial, influential, good-natured and sincere. He is a sweet singer and an excellent organist. His gospel songs are bright and many are very popular. He has edited more than twenty music books, some of which are : " Polished Pearls," " The Helping Hand " (associated with Mr. W. T. Giffe), "The Voice of Joy," "The Children's Hallelujah," "Gems and Jewels" (associated with Mr. J. H. Fillmore), "Christian Work-Songs," "The Beauty," "The Lightning Music Reader," "The Festival Glee Book," "The Wide-Awake Glee Book," "Knights Templar Melodies," etc. Some of his cantatas are: "Santa Claus and Family," "The New Year," "Bon-Bon Land," etc. He also has a Thorough Base Book. In addition to these books he contributed largely to song books edited by other authors, besides writing a number of songs in sheet form.

Among his many popular gospel songs we mention the following: "The Celestial City," "Keep Step Ever," "Little Feet, Be Careful," "Zion, Lovely Zion," "The Rock and the Sand," "Rowing Against the Tide," "Jesus is Calling To-day," and many others.

In addition to his musical contributions, Mr. Rosecrans has contributed to various religious papers, etc.

Few men have done more difficult, patient, skillful, efficient Christian work in the last thirty or more years than Mr. Rosecrans. Perhaps the chief cause of his well-earned distinction is attributable to his long and valuable services in the field of sacred music. Hundreds of persons have been brought into the church through his inspiring gospel songs and evangelistic labors.

W. L. THOMPSON.

XLI

Will L. Thompson

THE subject of this sketch was one of America's most popular song writers. His music has found its way into every nook and corner of the singing world. It would be difficult to find a person who sings who is not familiar with some of his compositions.

Will Lamartine Thompson was born at East Liverpool, Ohio, November 7, 1847. His father, the Hon. Josiah Thompson, was a successful business man, and for two terms a member of the state legislature. All the family were lovers of music, but Will Lamartine alone made it a serious study. He readily learned to play on instruments and even while a boy was in demand as pianist for local concerts. When he was only sixteen years old he composed "Darling Minnie Gray" and "Liverpool Schottische," both of which were published.

He was educated in the public schools of the town. Later he attended Union College.

In the years 1870–1873, he attended the Boston Music School, where he took a course in piano, organ and harmony. Near the close of his work here he wrote a song which, when published, almost immediately attained great popularity. That song was "Gathering Shells From the Seashore."

Mr. Thompson also studied in Germany. Music seemed to be his natural element.

In 1874 he took four of his songs in manuscript to a well-known publisher in Cleveland and offered all for one hundred dollars. He was informed by the publisher that the four pieces were not worth at the outside more than twenty-five dollars. After thinking the matter over for some time, he decided to take his songs back home with him. Later he had his songs published in New York City, but managed the sales himself. All the songs had a good sale, but two of them, " Gathering Shells From the Seashore " and " Drifting With the Tide," became immensely popular. In less than a year the publisher who had refused to pay one hundred dollars for the manuscripts had turned over to the author in profits more than a thousand dollars. From this initial venture his financial returns were most gratifying. Thus began what afterwards developed into the flourishing and popular firm—Will L. Thompson & Co.

Mr. Thompson's chief ambition was to write music for the people ; in this he was eminently successful.

A friend once said to Mr. Thompson : " How do you go about writing a song ? "

Opening a folio of manuscripts he replied : " You see here perhaps fifty or more manuscripts in various degrees of completion. Most of them are unfinished, and some merely contain the idea or theme. Others, you see, are almost ready for publication. I carry with me always a pocket memorandum, and no matter where I am, at home or hotel, at the store or in the cars, if an idea or theme comes to me that I deem worthy of a song, I jot it down in verse, and as I do so the music simply comes to me naturally, so I write words and music enough to call back the whole theme again any time I open to it. In this way I never lose it. I sat down one day at the seashore, and in about ten minutes wrote words and music of ' Gathering Shells From the Seashore.' I sat in a little boat one afternoon at Chautauqua Lake, and while my companion rowed through the lily beds I wrote ' Come, Where the Lilies Bloom.' So you see the surroundings generally suggest the theme."

" But how do you get the music in your mind without going to the instrument ? "

" That is hard to explain to any but a musician. The music comes to my mind the same as any other thought. As I write the words of a song, a fitting melody is already in my mind, and as I jot down the notes of the music I know just how it will sound. I write the different parts of the harmony and the whole piece is rehearsed in my mind ; I hear the blending of the different voices and know just how each part will sound in its harmonic relations to the other parts. Of course to do this intelligently, one must have a knowledge of the science of harmony, as there are rules governing the harmonic relations of sounds just as arbitrary as the rules of mathematics."

Mr. Thompson was a successful business man as well as a talented and successful composer, and his work brought him a fortune of which any composer or literary man might well be proud. In addition to scores of songs published in sheet form, he also issued a number of books, entitled as follows: " Thompson's Class and Concert," " Thompson's Popular Anthems, Vols. 1 and 2," " The New Century Hymnal," " The Young People's Choir," and "Enduring Hymns." These books have all met with general favor. Among his many popular gospel songs are: "There's a Great Day Coming," "Softly and Tenderly," "The Sinner and Song," "Lead Me Gently Home, Father," "Jesus is All the World to Me," etc.

Mr. Thompson was a good man, kind, quiet, unassuming, and one who was greatly loved and admired.

In 1891, Mr. Thompson married Miss Elizabeth Johnson, a lady of culture and refinement. Their home at East Liverpool, Ohio, is one of elegance and beauty.

In 1909, Mr. and Mrs. Thompson and their son made a tour through Europe. On their return trip Mr. Thompson was stricken with pneumonia. On reaching New York, he was taken at once to the Presbyterian Hospital, where he died September 20, 1909. His remains were taken to East Liverpool for burial.

E. E. REXFORD.

XLII

E. E. Rexford

EBEN E. REXFORD was born at Johnsburgh, N. Y., July 16, 1848. When about eight years old, his parents moved to Wisconsin, where he has since resided.

When quite young his talent for versification made itself evident. His first attempts at verse-writing were published in a New York paper. When about sixteen he received his first check for literary work, and that decided for him the choice of literature as a profession. Up to that time he had received only such educational training as the common schools afford. With a view to fitting himself for larger usefulness in the field he had chosen for himself, he entered Lawrence University, at Appleton, Wis., and paid his way through school by writing stories and poems for the eastern magazines. It was while he was in college that Mr. H. P. Danks, of New York, wrote him asking for song-words, which some one had told the composer he had the "knack" of writing. Mr. Danks offered to pay three dollars for each song he accepted. Mr. Rexford sent him nine, and subsequently he was paid eighteen dollars for six of them, and the other three were never accounted for. One of the songs sent was "Silver Threads Among the Gold," which gained world-wide popularity, as set to music by Mr. Danks. Mr. Rexford, in telling the story of this song, often says that he doesn't know whether it brought him three dollars or nothing since he has no means of knowing whether it was one of the six paid for or one of the three which were lost.

Mr. Rexford first heard the song sung under rather peculiar circumstances. He was aware that it had been published, but he had never seen it. While on a visit home, during vacation, a company of Oneida Indians from the reservation near Green Bay gave a concert in Shiocton. He attended this, and heard his song sung for the first time, little thinking that it was destined to prove one of the most popular ever written.

Previous to this, he had written several songs for Dr. Geo. F. Root, the well-known Chicago composer. These were published in books edited by Dr. Root, and in sheet form, and those of a sacred character soon attracted attention, and the demand came for more. As nearly as he can remember, the first one to become popular was "The Beacon Light." Others followed in rapid succession, among them, "O, Where Are the Reapers?" one of the most popular of Sunday-school songs. As originally written, the title of this song was, "O, We Are the Reapers." Mr. Root showed the song as he had set it to Mr. Sankey, who was then beginning his gospel-song work in connection with Mr. Moody, and expressed the opinion that it could be made useful in evangelistic work. Mr. Sankey agreed with him, but when he talked the matter over with Mr. Moody the latter objected to the title, because it would seem as if the use of the word "we" carried with it the idea that they were the "great and only" reapers in the field. At his suggestion the title was changed to "O Where," etc.

Since then Mr. Rexford has written a great many

songs of similar character for such composers as Root, Murray, Sankey, Excell, Gabriel, and others who have furnished music for the standard hymnology of the day. His work will be found in nearly all collections of sacred music.

Hymn-writing has been a side issue with him, however. His stories and poems have been published in many of the leading magazines east and west, and his articles of floriculture have secured for him positions on nearly all the household magazines in an editorial capacity. For fourteen years he had charge of the floricultural department of the *Ladies' Home Journal*, and is now doing similar work on *American Homes and Gardens, House and Garden*, and *American Home Monthly*, while independent articles along this line are constantly being contributed to leading periodicals. The late Peter Henderson said: "Mr. Rexford has done more to make flower-growing popular than all the rest of us put together"—high praise, coming from such a source, and a tribute of which the author is justly proud. For some years he was connected with James Vick, whose name was a household word among flower-loving people, as a contributor to *Vick's Magazine*, and it was while doing work on this periodical that his first book, "Home Floriculture," was published. Since then he has published "Flowers—How to Grow Them," "Four Seasons in a Garden," "The Home Garden," and a new book, called "Indoor Gardening," is now on the press.

Mr. Rexford has never published his miscellaneous poems in book form, but some years ago he brought out a story in verse, "Brother and Lover," which has sold steadily ever since, and gains in popularity with each succeeding year. It is a story of war-time, and has in it the heart-interest which seems to characterize most of this author's work along poetical lines.

Mr. Rexford is very happily married, and has a beautiful home in the fine little town of Shiocton, Wis. He has been organist of the Congregational Church in that place for over twenty years. Two years ago his *alma mater*, in recognition of his work along literary lines, conferred on him the degree of Doctor of Literature.

Mr. Rexford has written quite a number of secular songs which have been popular, especially several set to music by the late Harrison Millard, among which "The Two Pictures" and "The Ebbing Tide" are best known. Another, "Only a Pansy Blossom," was very popular some years ago.

Many of his best sacred songs have been set to music for the special use of prominent singers in church work, and he has furnished English words for some of the most popular operatic airs for this purpose for eastern musicians. Dr. Rexford's gospel poems have greatly enriched the hymnology of the church.

GEO. C. HUGG.

XLIII

George C. Hugg

GEORGE C. HUGG, son of the late John and Elizabeth Hugg, was born May 23, 1848, near Haddonfield, N. J. His earlier years were spent on a farm, and he received his education in the public schools. Being naturally musical, alone and unaided, he studied harmony and composition, and made fine progress. When only twelve years of age he became choirmaster of the Presbyterian Church at Berlin, N. J. He studied and practiced diligently at every opportunity, and when fourteen years old, his first song was published, entitled "Walk in the Light," and it became very popular, which greatly encouraged the young author.

Mr. Hugg was quite a prolific composer, and his compositions number over two thousand; eighteen books of revival and Sunday-school music, and about ninety song services for special occasions, such as Christmas, Easter, Children's Day, etc. Many of his songs have been reprinted in other books and translated into several different languages; thus they are sung largely over the world and are instrumental in leading many from the way of sin into Christ's Kingdom.

In 1891, Mr. Hugg was married to Miss Annie E. Ketchum, of Scullville, N. J., a lady of culture and intelligence, and a strong helper in her husband's publishing business.

Mr. Hugg had a rich baritone voice of wide range which enabled him to succeed both as a soloist and leader; he was also a good speaker, and did much Christian work in various places. He was for a number of years choirmaster of Tabernacle Presbyterian Church and Sunday-school, and Broad and Arch Street M. E. Church, Sunday-school, all of Philadelphia. He was closely connected with, and took active part in, Harper Memorial Presbyterian Church and Sunday-school, 29th Street and Susquehanna Avenue, same city. For over sixteen years he also held different offices, such as elder, deacon, trustee and assistant Sunday-school superintendent. Among the books published by Mr. Hugg we mention the following: "The Crowning Triumph," "Exalted Praise," "Temperance Light," "Bible Gems," "Golden Rays," "The Helper," "Laus Deo and Sacred Duets," "Sunlight in Sacred Song," "Rich in Blessing," "Heavens Echo," "On Wings of Song," "Echo and Blessing Combined," "Light in the Valley," "Songs of the Mercy-Seat," "Fairer than Day," "Corn in Egypt," and "The Royal Proclamation of Song."

Some of his most popular and widely known gospel songs are: "No, Not One," "Scatter Precious Seed," "Round the Pier," "We'll Never Say Good-Bye," "I Expect to Get to Heaven by the Same Old Way," "Take Off the Old Coat," "Beautiful Land of the Jasper Walls," "The Fire is Burning," "The Blood Upon the Door," "Anchored," "Jesus Never Leaves the Ship," "The Isle of Somewhere," "Gathering On the Hilltops of Glory," and "Satisfied." His only child inspired him to write one of his most beautiful hymns, which he entitled "Father Holds the Hand," and dedicated it to his " Evangeline."

Over one hundred thousand copies each of " Rich in Blessing " and " Light in the Valley " were sold. Two hundred and fifty thousand copies of Easter services were sold by a New York house in one season. Mr. Hugg was quite a successful composer and publisher in his line of work in Philadelphia. He was well known throughout New Jersey, Philadelphia, Central Pennsylvania, Delaware, and Maryland Methodist Episcopal Conferences, being associated with the musical part of a number of their different camp-meetings.

Mr. Hugg died October 13, 1907. A great worker in the vineyard of gospel song is gone, but many of his songs will live on and do good. Mrs. Hugg conducts the publishing business since the death of her husband. May success crown her every effort. She resides in Philadelphia. The gospel in song is one of the most effectual means of the age in reaching the unsaved, and evangelizing the world.

W. T. GIFFE.

XLIV

W. T. Giffe

WILLIAM THOMAS GIFFE was born at Portland, Indiana, June 28, 1848. Shortly after his birth his parents moved to a farm, only partly cleared. " W. T.," as he is familiarly called, remained until he was just sixteen when he entered the Union army and served as a soldier during the last year of the Civil War.

He was educated at Liver College (now extinct) and studied law for two years. In the meantime he had been a singer in the college glee club and had taken lessons in the college singing school. Later he studied with such teachers as Prof. J. W. Suffern, Dr. Geo. F. Root, Dr. L. O. Emerson, Dr. H. R. Palmer, and Dr. H. S. Perkins, in their normal music schools.

He was in much demand as a concert singer, having a fine baritone voice. He soon became popular as a chorus director and a convention conductor. Mr. Giffe's first book for singing schools was the " New Favorite," of which many thousands were sold. His books for male voices have been very popular; the same is true of his many anthem books.

The Oliver Ditson Company, Boston, Mass., are the publishers of several of his former books, but his later works are all published by The Home Music Company, Logansport, Ind., of which firm Mr. Giffe is the owner and proprietor. He is also the author of " A Practical

Course in Harmony and Musical Composition," one of the plainest and most complete harmony text-books of the present day. This book is now published by Theo. Presser, Philadelphia, Pa.

Mr. Giffe was editor and publisher of the *Home Music Journal* (now discontinued) for several years. He is an excellent writer.

He was supervisor of music in the public schools of his home city for a number of years. His work in the schools was a pronounced success. He resigned this work to engage in the publishing business.

He is the author of a number of gospel songs that have become favorites wherever used.

Mr. Giffe, wife and adopted daughter reside in Logansport, Ind., in one of the most beautiful residences in that city owned by himself. He is a man of unquestionable integrity and high standing. He is a fluent speaker and has been in frequent demand as a speaker on public occasions. He was one of three public men selected to deliver an address on the occasion of the late President McKinley Memorial Services held in Logansport on the day of the President's funeral.

His musical works, his teaching, his citizenship, his home and home life are a great credit to the music profession. For several years past he has done but little teaching, as his time is almost wholly occupied in his real estate business, and the supervision of the business of The Home Music Company. His home is noted for its hospitality, where musical people always are sure of a warm welcome.

Prof. W. T. Giffe is a talented man, and a gentleman who has done much good musical work. May he live long and continue to let his musical light shine.

J. H. FILLMORE.

XLV

J. H. Fillmore

JAMES HENRY FILLMORE was born in Cincinnati, Ohio, June 1, 1849. He is the eldest of a family of seven children, five sons and two daughters. The parents of this musical family were Rev. A. D. Fillmore, a minister of the Christian Church, and a musical author and publisher of note in his day, and Hannah M. Fillmore (née Lockwood), a singer of considerable fame in her time.

Three of the sons, J. H., Charles M., and Fred. A., have made their mark as composers, and have been a part of the Fillmore Brothers' music firm since young manhood. Frank has taught music classes, but at present is a farmer in Oklahoma. Aden L., the youngest, has made a reputation as an evangelistic singer, and for several years has taught music in the public schools in the suburbs of Pittsburgh, also conducting large chorus choirs in churches.

J. H. Fillmore, after going through the public schools of Cincinnati, learned the printing trade—typesetting, including music printing. At the time J. H. was twenty-one his father died, leaving the family on a small farm near Cincinnati. The father left also a little estate consisting of one or two church music books that were selling pretty well. J. H. decided to quit the printing-office and devote himself to teaching church congregational singing, using the books that his father had published.

He made a success of music teaching and music book selling, thereby supporting the family and educating the younger children. He soon revised the latest church music book of his deceased father, adding to it many of the later popular pieces, with some of his own writing, thereby greatly increasing its sale.

His first song book was "Songs of Glory," for Sunday-schools. He had invented a notation with figures in the notes. This book became very popular. Its large sales enabled him and his brother Frank to launch the firm of Fillmore Brothers, music publishers, which is now so well known. "Songs of Glory" was issued in 1874 and was followed by "Hours of Song" for singing schools which sold largely, and, surprising as it may seem, is still having a good sale.

From this beginning grew one of the most influential music publishing houses in the country. In the lines of church and Sunday-school music, gospel songs, day-school songs, anthems, choruses, temperance and prohibition songs and general sheet music, the firm has for years occupied a foremost position. Several years ago a monthly music journal, called *The Musical Messenger* and edited by Chas. M. and J. H. Fillmore, was published by the firm. It was the most popular magazine of its day with teachers and amateurs. *The Musical Messenger* has, in recent years, been changed to a band and orchestra journal, with a large circulation.

While Mr. Fillmore has been all these years at the head of the Fillmore Brothers' Music House, he has also written music voluminously. The books that he has edited and helped edit run up into the hundreds, both large and small. In addition he has kept up an annual issue of services or concert exercises for Sunday-schools for Christmas, Easter, Children's Day and other special occasions.

He has always been an active church and Sunday-school worker, leading the music and serving as a church officer in his home congregation. He has also been a prominent figure in the national gatherings of his denomination, often leading the music at its conventions, and has been honored by his brethren with positions on their missionary boards.

Mr. Fillmore was one of the founders of The Protestant Home for Working Boys in Cincinnati, an institution for taking care of orphan boys. It was started in 1899 and is still in a flourishing condition, having graduated into honorable manhood many boys who might otherwise have perished. From the beginning of the Home Mr. Fillmore has been an honored trustee and the active treasurer of the institution. He has also been a liberal contributor to the Home as well as to many other worthy benevolences. In fact, much of the money that Mr. Fillmore has earned has found its way into the various departments of church activities and other benevolent institutions.

While Mr. Fillmore has never been a politician in the popular sense of the term, he, feeling his responsibility as a citizen, has always been deeply interested in good government; and has ever been active and persistent in his earnest advocacy of all moral reforms. In his conscientious views of righteous government he has not always been "the stronger on the stronger side," but has never yielded his convictions nor his persistence. Though singularly without malice or partisan bias, he has ever had the courage of his convictions, and has never feared nor failed to lift his voice and use his pen in behalf of what he conscientiously felt to be right in political, social or religious matters.

Mr. Fillmore's health was never robust. He has been rather a delicate and overworked man, and has passed through some financial and physical trials that have hindered him for a time; but now, in his sixty-second year, his health is better than it ever was, and he is doing more and better work than at any period of his life. He does not seem to know that there is such a thing as a "dead line" this side of the tomb. Every one who knows him expects him to live as long as Gladstone or Fanny Crosby, and to be just as virile as the former, and as unfading and unfailing as the latter, to the last.

Personally, Mr. Fillmore is congenial, liberal and companionable. He is well beloved by all who know him. He is not rich in this world's goods because he has been generous. He has handled a good deal of money in his time, and much that he has personally earned has been banked in heaven where he hopes some day to find it.

This sketch would not be complete without mention of the home-life of Mr. Fillmore. To him the precincts of home have ever been sacred, and here in the bosom of his interesting family he has found inspiration, encouragement, happiness and rest. Here he is cherished, honored and loved. His home calls out his utmost fidelity and devotion, his loyalty and love.

He was happily married thirty-one years ago. He and his wife before their marriage were teachers in the Sunday-school together. It has always been a question of debate as to which is the most popular of the two. Their home has been the hospitable abiding place of preachers, missionaries and prominent people of their church, as well as the stopping place for their large circle of relatives and friends. In other words, they have always been entertainers in their home. They have four living children. The oldest, Henry Fillmore, is a band and orchestra musician and composer. He is now associated with The Fillmore Music House, having an office in the building. His special work is writing and arranging band and orchestra music, both sacred and secular. He writes not only under his own name, but under a *nom de plume* or two, and it is not an exaggeration to say that his band and orchestra music is as popular as any published. His special band instrument is the slide trombone. He has written some trombone humoresques that are standard concert numbers. Their daughter Mary is married to Mr. S. C. Shipley, a professor in the University of Minnesota. They live in their own home in Minneapolis. Freddie, the second daughter, named after her uncle, Fred. A., is a fine pianist and singer. The baby daughter, Annie Louise, graduated from the Norwood (Cincinnati) High School, June, 1911. She is a talented, all-round musician as well as a popular teacher and leader among her set.

This world has been made happier and better because James H. Fillmore lived in it. The sunshine of his nature has scattered many a cloud, and made radiant many a face, and gladdened many a heart. His beautiful songs have been sung over all this fair land of ours, and their sweet strains still echo and will re-echo down the ages. His songs have been sung and are sung to-day in stately cathedral, village church and humble cottage home with equal fervor, pleasure and profit. Because of his songs many a church is richer in grace and spirituality; and many an individual has a firmer grasp upon God and His promises, and upon purity and the sweeter and better things of life. Many have heard in these gospel songs the sweet invitation of Jesus, and turned from a life of sin to find peace and the Saviour's pardoning love. Countless throngs of the young have sung Fillmore's matchless children's songs. How these bright and beautiful songs for the children have enriched the music of our Sunday-schools and gladdened youthful hearts on Children's Day! How these songs have thrilled us all and helped us all to help others!

Mr. Fillmore has edited and published two church hymnals that compare favorably with the best in the land. His musical compositions are always practical, singable, and most of them possess a merit that gives them long life. Some of his most popular gospel songs are: "I am Resolved," "I Know that My Redeemer Liveth," "Tell It To-day," "Purer in Heart," "Only Waiting," "Victory Ours Shall Be," "The Victory May Depend on You," "Going Down the Valley," "I've Wandered Oft," "He Stands So Near," or "He Waits for Thee," "Would You Have the Joy Bells?" "Calling Me Over the Tide," "No More Good-Byes," etc.

" Sing unto the Lord, bless His name; show forth His salvation from day to day."

FRED. A. FILLMORE.

XLVI

Fred. A. Fillmore

FREDERICK AUGUSTUS FILLMORE, the subject of this sketch, was born in Paris, Ill., May 15, 1856. His father, A. D. Fillmore, was a preacher, music teacher, composer and author of quite a number of church music books. He had a voice of wonderful compass and sweetness, and as an effective gospel singer he was unequalled in his day. Mr. Fred. Fillmore's mother, Hannah Lockwood Fillmore, possessed rare musical talent, and a sweet, sympathetic voice.

The five boys and two girls (all living) born of these richly endowed parents became heirs, naturally and abundantly, to this great talent. And from their birth to maturity they were reared in an atmosphere of music.

The family moved from Paris, Ill., to Cincinnati, Ohio, when Fred. was quite young. Later his father bought a small farm near Terrace Park, a beautiful suburb of Cincinnati, where he moved his family. Fred. was always a great lover of the country and this change from city to country life proved to be quite a health tonic for the delicate lad.

His early struggles in life were parallel with many others who have made a name and fame for themselves. A great calamity to him and the family was the death of his father, a few years after moving to the country.

This left the mother and six children dependent on the eldest brother, J. H., senior member and founder of The Fillmore Bros. Co., music publishers of Cincinnati and New York. It was not long after this, however, until Fred. A. was able to help support himself and the younger children of the family by working on a farm for wages.

He attended the public schools in the country where he lived, which were exceptionally good. About this time his musical talent began to develop. He would spend every moment of spare time at the piano or organ, improvising, picking out melodies and learning to play the hymns and songs of the church and Sunday-school.

A brass band was organized at Milford, a town about a mile from his home. The leader asked Fred. to join, which he did, for he was one of that kind of boys who would at any time run a mile to hear a band play. The leader gave him some instruction and a band book, and he practiced so diligently that within a week he could play his part to every piece on the tuba. He then practiced the baritone and soon became an efficient soloist.

Later an opportunity presented itself to him for entering college, which he did, and worked his way through school by teaching vocal music in the college. Here he composed his first song which was sung by the college class at the commencement exercises. There being a good teacher of the piano in the school he took a course of lessons, and put in every moment of spare time in systematic practice. On leaving college he spent about six months teaching singing classes in the country, after which he spent some time in the study of harmony and composition, and began his career as a composer of music. Taking the field again as singing class teacher, having qualified himself as a teacher of the organ and piano in connection with the singing class work, he always had pupils enough to keep him busy. In teaching over a wide territory in the states of Ohio, Indiana, Kentucky, Tennessee, Alabama, Missouri and Pennsylvania, he carried with him energy, enthusiasm and a high moral purpose that made his work everywhere·a success. This practical work and learning the needs of the people induced him to write his first book, " Banner of Beauty," a well arranged book for singing classes, which was a success from the start, and established the reputation of its author.

In his experience as a teacher of the piano and organ (the organ more especially), he found very little music especially adapted to the use of the parlor organ, so he conceived the idea of writing music to meet this demand.

In January, 1891, The Fillmore Brothers began the publication of *The Musical Messenger*, a monthly journal of literature and music. Fred. A. contributed to this magazine easy pieces for the organ and piano, and his marches, waltzes, etc., especially those adapted to the organ, sprang at once into popular favor. To more fully meet the needs and demands of the people, Mr. Fillmore prepared " The New Practical Organ Instructor." This is an excellent work and has sold by the thousands.

During all this time he was writing gospel and Sunday-school songs. His songs are to be found in all the leading gospel song books of the day. His two books for the Sunday-school, " Songs of Rejoicing " and "Heart Songs," are very popular. His two books of anthems, "Triumphant Praise" and "Anthem Praise," also show that Professor Fillmore is an excellent composer of this class of music.

As has already been stated, he is a great lover of the country. He was also a lover of the country girls, and married the one of his choice, bought the old homestead, where he still resides happy and contented with his wife and interesting family of two boys and two girls.

Here during the long winter months he puts in the time writing anthems, gospel songs, Sunday-school songs, Easter and Christmas exercises.

Some of his best inspirations came from farm experiences, as some of his widely known popular songs show—"Are You Sowing the Seed of the Kingdom?" "Scatter Seeds of Loving Deeds," "Are You Sowing the Seed Over Soil Rich and Fertile?" and "Hast Thou Sown the Precious Seed?"

Some of his friends call him "the farmer musician," a title he accepts with becoming pride. He considers his best compositions are "Old Home Songs," a medley, a song picturing the home life, and a reminiscence of the Fillmore family, and "The Bible That My Mother Used to Read," a solo and chorus, which is very popular.

He is an active worker in his home church, and his influence is ever for righteousness, godliness and Christian living.

REV. CHAS. M. FILLMORE.

XLVII

Rev. Charles M. Fillmore

THE gentleman that we now present is one of the ministers whose career is worthy of the highest commendation. He comes from a musical family, his mother being considered a beautiful singer in her day, and his father, Augustus D. Fillmore, was a pioneer preacher, musical composer, teacher and publisher. The son seems to have inherited his father's most striking characteristics.

Charles Millard Fillmore was born in Paris, Ill., July 15, 1860. He began the study of music in his boyhood days, and grew up in a musical atmosphere. His first piano teacher was the veteran Henry D. Sofge. He graduated from the Woodward High School in 1881. While a pupil in this school, five free scholarships in the Cincinnati College of Music were offered each year to students of the high school excelling in competitive examinations. In a class of about one hundred, he was one of the five to carry off the honor, and he spent a year in this great music school. He then taught for one year in Bath Seminary, Owingsville, Ky., having charge of the music and literary branches. Then for about a year he travelled and taught singing classes in various parts of the country. In order to gain a more thorough knowledge of music he returned to Cincinnati, and continued his study of piano, harmony and composition, under the celebrated teacher, Arthur Mees. Mr. Fillmore then spent some time teaching, leading church choirs, conducting choral societies, writing music, contributing articles to various magazines, and making himself useful in many ways.

Early in life he joined the Christian Church, and felt an inclination towards the ministry, and with this high purpose in view he entered Butler College, Irvington, Ind., and took a regular classical course in addition to his Biblical work, and graduated in 1890, with the degree of Bachelor of Arts. He deserves the credit of " making his way " through college by teaching music, and also by preaching for country churches around Indianapolis. He also conducted the music in the chapel, and was one of the editors of the *Butler Collegian*.

Since graduation he has been continuously engaged in Christian work in various parts of the country. He was pastor at Lafayette, Ind., two years ; Shelbyville, one year ; State Evangelist, one year ; Ogden, Utah, as missionary supply, six months ; Peru, Ind., nearly six years ; Carthage, Ohio, eight years. At present he is pastor at Hillside, Indianapolis, Ind. Mr. Fillmore is meeting with excellent success, building up large congregations, and an occasional church building.

He is one of the editors of *Clean Politics*, a reform paper devoted especially to national Prohibition. The circulation is already nearing the 100,000 mark. He is also literary editor of *The Choir*. He had editorial charge of *The Musical Messenger* during the six years it was published. In nearly all of the leading church and Sunday-school books may be found hymns and songs, both words and music of his composition.

When Rev. Chas. M. Fillmore wrote the song, "Tell Mother I'll Be There," he seems to have struck the heart-strings of all humanity, which have vibrated around the world.

Mr. Chas. M. Alexander, the world-famous singing evangelist, says, "'Tell Mother I'll Be There' has converted more men than any other song written in a decade. A song which critics have tried to cut to pieces, both words and music, but I have never found a song which would take its place. One night in Liverpool while the choir was singing 'Tell Mother I'll Be There,' one hundred and sixty men arose and publicly accepted Christ before all the people."

Every man and woman who sings or hears this song instantly recalls the home of childhood and that one above all others who made that place—"Home, Sweet Home."

Mr. Fillmore is happily married, and in their home they have three daughters. May he be permitted to live long and write many more inspiring songs that will lift human souls to God.

MRS. E. L. ASHFORD.

XLVIII

Mrs. E. L. Ashford

EMMA LOUISE ASHFORD was born March 27, 1850, in the state of Delaware, of English parents. Her father was a music teacher, and from him she received her first instruction. Her mother was possessed of a beautiful soprano voice. Emma could sing from childhood, even before she could speak plainly. Music was a part and parcel of her home life. When she was three years of age she sang a solo at a charity concert. At the age of five she began to extemporize altos to the songs and hymns her mother sang; and then sang trios with her parents. Her father gave her short lessons daily in sight reading, and at the end of six months she was able to sing correctly the alto parts of hymns and anthems without the aid of an instrument. At the age of eight years she was admitted into the village church choir, and also the glee club as alto, and was acknowledged to be the best sight reader in the choir or club. Her father was director of both organizations.

When she was ten years old a guitar was presented to her, which afforded her great joy. In a few weeks she could play the accompaniments to the songs she sang. By this time she was a good performer on the piano and organ.

When fourteen years of age, she moved with her

parents to Plymouth, Mass. Here her guitar playing
created quite an interest; and she taught a class of
young ladies, and also sang in a choir. The following
year they moved to Seymour, Conn. Here she was offered the position as organist in St. Peter's (Episcopal)
Church. This was her first experience in playing the
pipe organ, and after a year's service resigned to take
a larger organ at an advanced salary. While in Seymour she studied the piano with Mrs. Street, and the
pipe organ with the late Dr. Anderson.

When a little past seventeen, she was married to
Mr. John Ashford. (Her maiden name was Hindle.)
Mr. Ashford had a fine tenor voice, which greatly assisted him in capturing his prize. Soon after their marriage they went to Chicago, where she had the honor
of holding the position of alto in the quartet of St.
James (Episcopal) Church, the organist and director at
that time being the late Dudley Buck, who gave her
the preference over twenty-seven other applicants. To
be associated week after week with such a great musician as Professor Buck was in itself a liberal education; and from a musical standpoint, Mrs. Ashford
considers this to have been the most important year
of her life. At the close of the year her husband accepted a position in Nashville, Tenn., in which city
they still reside.

Mrs. Ashford and her husband were associated together in choir work for many years. For ten years
they had charge of the music in a Presbyterian Church
and the Jewish Temple simultaneously. On account of
failing health she finally gave up choir work. Mrs.
Ashford taught piano and organ for twenty years; but
also gave that up in order to spend all of her time in

musical composition; in this, as well as her choir work and teaching, she has been eminently successful. Mrs. Ashford studied advanced harmony, counterpoint, canon and fugue, with Dr. R. H. Peters, an English musician, and also with other teachers.

Her first work of importance in the line of composition was seventeen anthems which she contributed to E. O. Excell's book of anthems. Calls came from other publishers, and she was soon kept busy.

In 1894 she visited Europe, where she devoted the greater part of her time studying the higher forms of ecclesiastical music. On her return she began writing for Mr. Lorenz, and won the first prize in an anthem contest which he conducted. At the suggestion of Mr. Lorenz, she wrote her first sacred cantata, "The Prince of Peace." She made another visit abroad in 1897, and again in 1904. These visits were principally to view the wonders of the old world, and listen to its fine church music.

In 1900 the Vanderbilt University celebrated its twenty-fifth anniversary; and for this occasion Mrs. Ashford was asked to compose an Ode, which was rendered by a chorus of eighty voices and an orchestra of twenty-five performers. She has written quite a number of songs for the university glee club; and in recognition of this work she was presented a beautiful cup, suitably engraved.

Several years ago Mrs. Ashford became connected with The Lorenz Publishing Company, of Dayton, Ohio. She speaks in the highest terms of her appreciation of the unvarying kindness and encouragement which said company have given her in her musical work. She is also thankful for her many other loyal and appreciative coterie of friends, both men and women of large mind and broad culture who have ever stood ready to help her with words of wisdom and encouragement.

Mrs. Ashford is a very prolific writer, and her compositions rank with the best in their line. The following is a partial list of her published works: Two hundred and fifty anthems; fifty sacred solos; ten sacred duets; six sacred trios; eight sacred cantatas; two hundred organ voluntaries; "Ashford's Organ Instructor" (in five volumes); a large number of gospel songs; also two secular cantatas; a number of part-songs; forty teaching pieces for piano, and a number of secular solos. Much of her music is republished in England, and a Song Cycle called "Destiny" has recently been published in Germany.

May Mrs. Ashford be permitted to live long and continue to contribute of her musical genius to the world, and to His glory.

DR. D. B. TOWNER.

XLIX

Dr. D. Brink Towner

THE subject of this sketch, Daniel B. Towner, was born March 5, 1850, at Rome, Pa., where he was reared, and received an academic education. His father, Prof. J. G. Towner, was a singer and a music teacher of quite a reputation, and it was from him that the son received his early musical training.

At the age of seventeen he was exploited through Pennsylvania, southern New York and eastern Ohio as "the wonderful boy bass," appearing in many concerts where he sang the popular bass solos of the day, such as "Rocked in the Cradle of the Deep," "The Old Sexton," "Down by the Sea," "The King and the Miller," etc., etc. A few years later he began to teach vocal music and conduct musical institutes and conventions. He also gained quite a reputation as an oratorio baritone soloist. During the years .that he was thus engaged he was studying music with such men as John Howard, of New York, Dr. Geo. F. Root, of Chicago, Geo. Jas. Webb, of Boston, and others.

From his early youth he had dreams of some day being a composer and began to write songs and anthems even before he had studied harmony. Like many of our modern gospel song writers he began by writing secular songs, some humorous, and some sentimental. But as he became more actively engaged in the conducting of church music, these gave way for the gospel songs which have made him so widely known.

In December, 1870, Mr. Towner was married to Miss Mary E. McGonigle, who was a beautiful singer, and they soon settled in Binghamton, N. Y., where he had charge of the music in the Centenary M. E. Church. During these years he was an ardent student and conducted many musical institutes and conventions in connection with his church work.

In the fall of 1882 he located in Cincinnati, Ohio, where for two years he had charge of the music in the York Street M. E. Church. He was then called to the Union M. E. Church of Covington, Ky., where he remained until the fall of 1885, when he joined Dwight L. Moody in evangelistic work, conducting the music and singing solos in that connection in most of the large cities of the United States and Canada. He also had charge of the music for several years at the College Students' Conference at Mount Hermon and Northfield, Mass. In the fall of 1893 he assumed the superintendency of the music in the Moody Bible Institute, Chicago, where by his ability as an organizer and teacher he has succeeded in establishing one of the most unique and prosperous training schools for gospel singers in the world. It can be confidently said that most of the noted gospel singers of the present day have either been trained by, or have had personal contact with, Dr. Towner.

In September, 1900, the degree of Music Doctor was conferred upon him by the University of Tennessee. Dr. Towner is one among the world's most prolific gospel song writers. He has published more than two thousand compositions, and this only represents a part of his work as a musical composer. He has edited in part, or wholly, fourteen books, three of which have been for male voices and one for female voices.

His songs have literally belted the world, and are to be found in most of the hymn and tune books both in America and the British Empire. In more recent years he has spent considerable time in Great Britain in connection with large evangelistic meetings and prominent churches in London, Manchester, Dublin, Belfast, Dundee, and Edinburgh.

Dr. Towner is also by common consent one of the greatest evangelistic singers and leaders living. His ability to lead a great chorus and congregation is unsurpassed, while as a teacher of gospel songs and composer he stands in the front rank.

The following are a few of his most popular compositions: " Anywhere With Jesus," " Trust and Obey," " Paul and Silas," " Redeemed," " Nor Silver Nor Gold," " Saving Grace," " The Hand that Was Wounded for Me," " Full Surrender," " Would You Believe," " Only a Sinner," " Victory in My Soul," " Look and Live," " God's Skies are Blue," " Grace that is Greater Than Our Sin," " Love Took Him to the Cross," etc.

Dr. Towner has accomplished a great work for God and humanity, and we hope he may be spared for many more years of usefulness.

E. O. EXCELL.

L

E. O. Excell

ALL of the noted evangelists have perceived the great power of music upon the hearts of men and women to move them to action, to fill them with enthusiastic zeal for truth and holiness. Therefore they conceived the idea of making a specialty of sacred song, and thus began the distinctive work of the evangelistic singer. Hymns and music that are full of gospel truth and sentiment, and sung " with the spirit and understanding," wield a powerful influence for good over humanity and are sure to make their impress.

What would Moody have been without Sankey, Whittle without Bliss, Jones without Excell, Torrey and Chapman without Alexander, or any other one of the popular evangelists of the day without his singing companion ? Certainly they would have exerted some influence, but they all freely concede that much of the success of their work was and is due to the influence of gospel song as directed and interpreted by their singing companions. Perhaps there is no one better known and more popular as an evangelistic singer and gospel song composer, than the subject of this sketch, Edwin Othello Excell. He was born in Stark County, Ohio, December 13, 1851. His father, Rev. J. J. Excell, has been a good singer in his day and is a minister in the German Reformed church. The son served his apprenticeship and worked as plasterer and bricklayer for twelve years.

In 1871 Mr. Excell began teaching country singing schools, in which he was quite successful. This year was also made memorable by his marriage to Miss Jennie Bell, daughter of Hon. A. W. Bell, of East Brady, Pa. For a time Mr. Excell resided in East Brady, and had been engaged in singing campaign songs in not only the interest of the great general, U. S. Grant, but of his father-in-law who was also a candidate. About this time Rev. Dr. J. B. Espy, of East Brady M. E. Church, began a revival meeting and solicited the services of Mr. Excell to conduct the music. He responded to the call and under his leadership and stirring solos a great revival followed, Mr. Excell himself being one of the many converts. From this time on he devoted his energies to sacred song, and to more thoroughly equip himself for his chosen field of labor, he attended Dr. Root's normals in the years 1877–1883 inclusive, taking special voice training under Prof. F. W. Root.

In 1881 he was called to take charge of the choir at the First Methodist Church of Oil City, Pa., where he won new laurels, and remained there for a term of two years. In 1883 he moved to Chicago, where he still resides. Here he met Mr. B. F. Jacobs, the father and promoter of Sunday-school work. He and Bishop Vincent, of the Northern Methodist church, were the founders of the international Sunday-school lessons. For two years or more, Mr. Excell had charge of the music in the great Sunday-school work of Messrs. B. F. and W. B. Jacobs.

He then met Rev. Sam P. Jones, and in association

with him he worked for twenty years in all of his
revival meetings. He was with him in the last meeting
he ever held, which was in Oklahoma City. In their
labors they toured America, and were eminently successful. The great amount of good accomplished in
the evangelistic field by these two men will never be
fully known this side of eternity.

Mr. Excell has conducted the music in the State
Sunday-school Conventions in nearly every state and
territory in the United States, also in many of the
provinces of Canada. He has toured across the continent twice with Mr. Marion Lawrence, General
Secretary of the International Sunday-school Association. He has also been associated in Sunday-school
work with Rev. F. B. Meyer, the great London preacher,
Dr. Geo. W. Bailey, Bishop J. C. Hartzell, and many
others of world-wide fame. Besides this, he has directed
the music in many of the Chautauquas in various parts
of the country, and his efforts have been crowned with
success.

Professor Excell's fame does not rest entirely upon his
work in the evangelistic field. His beautiful gospel
songs alone would have made him famous. He has
composed between two and three thousand songs. A
few well known favorites are: " Since I Have Been
Redeemed," " God Calling Yet," " We Shall Stand
Before the King," " Let Him In," " Scatter Sunshine,"
" Count Your Blessings," " I Am Happy in Him," etc.

Then, too, he carries on quite an extensive publishing
business in Chicago, and has been very successful as a
business man as well as a singer and author. Professor
Excell has edited nearly fifty books for himself, and
thirty-eight for other parties.

The great popularity of his books is evidenced by the fact that, up to date, his gospel song and anthem books have reached the enormous sale of nearly ten million copies; and he is now selling from one and a quarter million to one and a half million books annually, and his book sales increase from year to year. Professor Excell is a very busy man and he has achieved great success in his chosen work.

His voice is a full, round baritone, of great volume, yet mellow and sweet. He sings with excellent taste and expression, and so has a moving influence over an audience, which is so essential to a successful evangelistic singer. He is yet in the vigor of manhood, and with his perfect health gives promise of living many years to bless the world with numerous compositions, and lead many souls to a decision for Christ and His service by the magnetic power of his matchless voice.

"Sing forth the honor of His name: make His praise glorious."

MRS. FLORA H. CASSEL.

LI

Mrs. Flora H. Cassel

WHEREVER gospel and temperance songs are sung the name of Mrs. Flora Hamilton Cassel is a familiar one. She was born at Otterville, Jersey County, Ill., August 21, 1852. (Her maiden name was Hamilton.) Most of her childhood was passed at Whitehall, Ill., where her father, Rev. B. B. Hamilton, was pastor of the Baptist church. She was quite musical from childhood, and could sing and play her own accompaniments when but a small girl.

When sixteen years of age, she went to live with her mother's sister, Mrs. Titcomb, in Brooklyn, N. Y. Here she continued her school work, and took lessons in voice culture of Madame Hartell, of New York City. Later her aunt sent her to Maplewood Institute, at Pittsfield, Mass., where she studied the piano, harmony and composition under Dr. B. C. Blodgett, and the voice under Prof. J. I. Lalor, taking also some of the academic branches of the school. Graduating from the musical department in 1873, she was engaged the next fall to teach, and take charge of the department of music, in Shurtleff College, Upper Alton, Ill. While here she was married to Dr. E. T. Cassel, of Nebraska City, Neb. Mrs. Cassel continued teaching in the college for a year or more. They then moved to Nebraska. While in that state, Dr. Cassel practiced medicine in South Bend, Ashland, Edgar, and Hastings; and in all these places Mrs. Cassel continued teaching, writing music and playing for the church choirs which her husband led.

It was while in Edgar that a Woman's Christian Temperance Union was organized with Mrs. Cassel at its head, and for many years the organization had her heartiest support. She organized her county, making it the banner county in the state, and was the first one in the organization to hold County W. C. T. U. Institutes.

During this period of public work she felt the need of special songs for temperance meetings, and this need gave birth to her song book, "White Ribbon Vibrations," which was published in 1890. The book became very popular; passed through many editions, and following the organization for which it was made, in every country in the world. Its initial song, Mrs. Cassel's words and music, now best known as "Around the World," was Frances Willard's favorite song. She made it the world's W. C. T. U. song, and had it sung at all her great meetings.

Soon after this publication, E. O. Excell, E. S. Lorenz, and others began publishing Mrs. Cassel's gospel songs, a number of which have become very popular.

When the first convention of the Baptist Young People's Union was to be held, the president of the State Union asked Mrs. Cassel to write a song for the occasion. Dr. Cassel took their motto for his theme, and wrote "Loyalty to Christ," and Mrs. Cassel wrote music for the hymn. It sprang into popularity at once, and became the National Christian Endeavor Song, and was also sung by the Epworth Leagues.

While Dr. Cassel was listening to a sermon about a

king's messenger, he took a card and wrote down the words of " The King's Business." Later a melody occurred to him as appropriate, and Mrs. Cassel arranged and harmonized it; thus the popular song, " The King's Business," was given to the world.

In 1893, Mrs. Cassel took advantage of an opening to go into the piano and organ business and continued in this steadily increasing business for nearly ten years. They then moved to Colorado, and purchased a farm near Denver—a delightful home with a magnificent view of mountain, plain and city. Mrs. Cassel has the oversight of her home interests. With her books and music, and composing beautiful gospel songs to further " the King's Business," she is one of the busiest and happiest women in the state of Colorado.

DR. J. B. HERBERT.

LII

Dr. J. B. Herbert

THE subject of this sketch, John Bunyan Herbert, was born at Cambridge, Ohio, September 14, 1852. The next year his parents moved to Monmouth, Ill., where he still resides. He early manifested an intense love for music and at the age of fourteen he bought a book on harmony, and with lofty aspirations bravely set to work to master it, all by himself, giving every spare moment to its study. And from that day to this his devotion to his art has brooked every obstacle, and his perseverance has brought him to his coveted position in life—that of a professional music writer.

He took a full literary course at the Monmouth College, and enjoys the distinction of being its first graduate. After his graduation, his father, ignoring his musical tastes and preferences, chose for him the medical profession, and sent him to the Hahnemann Medical College, at Chicago. But while there he continued his musical studies, and sang regularly in one of the church choirs. After three years at the medical college, he returned to Monmouth an M. D., and practiced the profession successfully for several years, still poring over his music books, however, when not responding to medical calls. He did not despise the medical profession, but he loved music more, and could not forsake it. In all these years he did not let a day pass without carefully writing one or more exercises in composition and harmony.

He toiled without the aid of an instructor, or even any one to sympathize with him or give him an encouraging word. But it shows his devotion to the art and the stuff he was made of, and as a result of this pluck and perseverance, he has developed within himself a mastery of the science that is enjoyed only by the few. His first encouragement came to him in the form of finding one of his songs printed, without the change of a note, in one of lamented Bliss' books, which he had modestly sent " to be published if found worthy."

In 1875 the light broke in fully upon him. Dr. Geo. F. Root and his son, Prof. Frederic W., held a normal in Monmouth, and our friend embraced the opportunity for all there was in it, especially the harmony and composition course taught by Prof. F. W. A strong and lasting friendship sprang up between them, and, after the normal closed, harmony lessons were continued by mail. The Doctor holds these great men in grateful remembrance for the good instruction received from them. He also studied with P. P. Bliss and others. His close and systematic study ultimately led him to victory.

His first published work was " Chapel Anthems," which appeared in 1878. During this year he discontinued his medical practice altogether, and determined to give his entire attention to music. The next year he travelled with Mr. J. C. Boutecue, a popular temperance lecturer, singing and conducting the singing for the meetings. While in this work he wrote a book of temperance songs. Also about this time his book,

"Herbert's Male Quartet Book," was issued. Then followed his class and convention book, "The Elite." Among the many books that followed we mention: "Bible Anthems," "Class and Concert," "Herbert's Anthems," "The Battle Cry," "Y. M. C. A. Gospel Songs," "Quaint Quartets," "Harp of David," "Christmas Anthem Collection," "Easter Anthem Collection," "Tabernacle Anthems," "Quartet Queen," "Herbert's Organ Voluntaries," "Glory Songs, New Gospel Hymn Book," "Voice Culture in Classes," "Class, Concert and Convention," etc. "Herbert's Harmony and Composition" and "How to Write an Accompaniment" are among the best theory works of their class, being clear and practical. The last named book has received many words of praise from both foreign and American musicians. Sir Frederic Bridge, organist of Westminster Abbey, England, spoke a good word for the work. Dr. Percy Goetschius, Dr. Emerson, Dr. Perkins and other American musicians have endorsed it. Dr. Herbert has other important musical works in preparation.

He is also in high favor as a singer and performer, a teacher, and a leader of conventions; he has also had much experience as organist and choir leader. However, he much prefers the more congenial work of musical composition in the quiet of his pleasant home. A musical critic, who is himself a composer of note, says: "The marked characteristic of all Dr. Herbert's music is its individuality." All his compositions show artistic design, and the details are all worked out with an elegance and finish that only masters of art can command. Many of his anthems, quartets and gospel songs are models of workmanship.

Dr. Herbert's musical works have good and steady sales and the royalties bring him a handsome income. He does but little or no teaching now, except he holds winter normals in the South. In this work he is doing great good for the cause of musical development, and his work is highly appreciated by those who have been in his theory and voice classes.

Dr. Herbert is a very modest and reserved gentleman. In society his sparkling wit and rare conversational powers make him a universal favorite. We hope he may live long and give to the world more of the rich gospel in song.

MRS. LAURA E. NEWELL.

LIII

Mrs. Laura E. Newell

THE subject of this sketch was born February 5, 1854, at New Marlborough, near Great Barrington, Mass., where her parents, Mr. and Mrs. Edward A. Pixley, resided, and where her mother died, leaving her a child in early infancy. A few months later her mother's aunt, then Mrs. Hiram Mabie, of New York, came to Massachusetts, and took the child home with her, and adopted her. She was a most faithful and devoted mother to her to the day of her death, which occurred in 1895, at her home in Zeandale, Kans.

When Laura was four years old, her foster parents removed to Kansas, and located south of the site on which Wamego now stands, and where Mr. Mabie engaged in farming. Two years later he died and her mother, who had been a very successful teacher in New York, resumed the work of teaching; however, under quite different conditions from her Eastern environments. There her schools were more advanced. But suffice it to say, her work was always well done, and " She hath done what she could " was the inscription her daughter had engraved on the granite that marks her resting place.

In 1860 Mrs. Mabie accepted a position in the city schools of Topeka, where she taught many years, and under her tutorship then and later the daughter received her education and training.

When a child of twelve years she wrote rhymes, spontaneously, we might say, and two years later her poems began to appear in the local newspapers. Still at that time no thought of a life-work with her pen dawned upon her mind. She simply wrote to give vent to her poetical mind, and as the years rolled by she kept on writing and gaining fame.

In 1871 she was married to Mr. Lauren Newell, a carpenter by trade. They reside at Manhattan, Kans.

It was in 1873 while Mrs. Newell was listening to an address by an able speaker, who spoke of the death of genuine hymns, that she resolved to try, and to test the merit, or de-merit of her ability in this line of work. Since that time her pen has been kept busy writing songs, sacred and secular, services for all anniversary occasions, cantatas, adapting words to music, and music to words. The orders have not ceased to keep her busy in filling them. Some of her poems have been translated into other languages. "What Will Your Record Be?" set to music by C. E. Leslie some twenty years ago, has long since appeared in many German publications both in this country and across the water.

Perhaps the most popular secular song (both words and music by Mrs. Newell) is "Across the Years," published in sheet form. Many other songs of hers are in sheet form. Calls from all parts of our land come to Mrs. Newell for poems, and she has been honored with orders from our very best composers, among which are: Dr. L. O. Emerson, Bartlett, Ogden, Herbert, Gabriel, Fillmore Bros., Parks, Hall, Leslie, Rosche, Lincoln, Westhoff, and scores of others.

Mrs. Newell is indeed a prolific writer. Her poems

number in the thousands. She has had over eight hundred poems published in a single year, a most remarkable record. The great ease with which Mrs. Newell writes is one of her special gifts. Not long since an order, accompanied by music and titles, was sent her for eight poems to suit. At seven o'clock in the evening she sat down to her organ to catch the music. Then she went to her desk, and at ten o'clock the order was ready for the return mail. Her work pleased the publisher so well that he sent her an order for forty-eight additional poems. Mrs. Newell writes several hundred poems annually.

She is a very modest and unpretentious lady, and goes about her daily work as cheerfully as her poems advise others to do. The deeply religious character of the woman stands out boldly in nearly all her work. The next world is apparently as real to her as the present. Her heart is in her work, and to the end of life's chapter, while able, may she wield her pen to tell the Story so dear to her heart, in verse and song.

E. S. LORENZ.

LIV

E. S. Lorenz

URING all ages music has been regarded as the handmaid of religion. The bards of old were co-workers with the prophets in cultivating the spiritual natures of the people. So it has followed naturally that while music has done much for religion, religion has also done much for music. With a desire to purify and elevate the music of God's sanctuary there has naturally come to many preachers of the Gospel the necessity of writing such songs as seemed to them suited to worship. Some ministers with special musical talent have found such a field of usefulness in this line that they have given up preaching to devote themselves entirely to the work of writing music, feeling that they could serve God and humanity as well in this way as in preaching. The subject of this sketch is one who is now devoting his life to sacred music, and he is preaching through gospel song to thousands of people all over the world, who otherwise would never hear his voice.

Edmund Simon Lorenz is the eldest son of Rev. Edward and Barbara (Gueth) Lorenz, and was born in Stark County, Ohio, July 13, 1854. Edmund attended the public schools in Stark County, in Cleveland and in Toledo, Ohio, and after graduating from the high school at the latter city engaged in teaching. Next he

entered Otterbein University, from which he graduated
with the degree of A. M. He was a student of Union
Biblical Seminary, of Dayton, Ohio, and later in Yale
Theological Seminary, from which he received the degree of Bachelor of Divinity. In 1883 and 1884 he
studied in the University at Leipzig, Germany, giving
special attention to philosophy and church history.

After his return from Europe he filled the pastorate
of High Street United Brethren Church in Dayton,
Ohio, for two years. In 1887 he was elected president
of Lebanon Valley College, at Annville, Pa. He entered upon this work with zeal and devotion, to which
was due great progress in the development and usefulness of the institution. But his physical constitution,
undermined by the double work of musical editing
and study during his collegiate and theological training, and the severity of his previous pastoral duties,
suddenly gave way in 1888, and he was completely
prostrated. The next three years were passed in weary
invalidism, and though his health is now excellent he
is still compelled to limit his public efforts and his enjoyment of general society. Shut out from public
work, he turned his attention to music, which had been
his diversion previously, and in the theory of which art
he had been thoroughly grounded.

Mr. Lorenz published his first book in 1875. Since
then he has edited fifty books which include Sunday-
school song books, gospel song books, hymnals and
anthem books, books for male voices and for primary
classes, services and cantatas, sheet music and even
organ music. His compositions are wholly of a religious character.

In 1886 Mr. Lorenz projected a series of books on

revival work, and in 1887 issued "The Coming Revival," a handbook for laymen ; also "The Gospel Worker's Treasury of Hymns and Revival Anecdotes," which contains suggestive revival texts, sermon outlines and Scripture readings, and this work is now a standard with preachers of all denominations. In 1888 appeared his "Getting Ready for a Revival," which also occupies a high place in revival literature. In 1909 Revell published his "Practical Church Music," an exhaustive study of principles, methods and plans in this neglected field. It is recognized as the leading book on this subject.

After somewhat recovering from his nervous collapse, Mr. Lorenz began the publication of sacred music in a small way under the firm name of Lorenz & Company, at Dayton, Ohio, and this firm is now, under the name of Lorenz Publishing Company, one of the leading houses in its line in the country, its trade extending from ocean to ocean, and into foreign lands. In 1894 he founded the *Choir Leader*, in 1897 the *Choir Herald*, monthly periodicals devoted to choir music, and now recognized as being the leading publications of their class in the world. The *Kirchenchor*, a German choir monthly, also edited by him, was founded in 1897. This business, with its New York branch, is steadily growing in extent, and is constantly broadening its scope.

While Mr. Lorenz, owing to his nervous limitations, left the ministry, he is still an active worker in church and Y. M. C. A. circles and makes a great many religious addresses of various kinds.

Mr. Lorenz resides in Dayton, Ohio, where he has a most pleasant home.

He is author of both words and music of many of his best gospel songs, and they are free from the commonplace jingle that has been too common in recent years. His songs show thought and a cultivated mind, and breathe a spirit of worshipful devotion that naturally commend them to those who desire to use music which can be sung "with the spirit and with the understanding also."

H. H. McGRANAHAN.

LV

H. H. McGranahan

THE subject of this sketch, H. H. McGranahan, was born at Jamestown, Pa., June 3, 1854. When he was ten years of age, he began the study of music under his uncle, James McGranahan, the eminent gospel song writer.

He commenced the study of theory and harmony in Dr. Geo. F. Root's Summer Normal School in 1875. These he attended regularly until 1881, excepting the summer of 1878, when he went to Europe with Dr. Eben Tourjee's musical party to the Paris Exposition, then making a tour through the principal countries of Europe.

For several years he was connected with Dr. H. R. Palmer's Summer School of Music as a pupil, also as a teacher of harmony and singing, and during the season conducted musical institutes and conventions in Pennsylvania, Ohio and New York.

He then entered the New England Conservatory of Music, Boston, studying voice culture with Lyman W. Wheeler and harmony and composition with J. C. D. Parker. In 1884 he taught in the New York City Church Choral Union, which was under Dr. H. R. Palmer's supervision, and in 1885 took charge of the same kind of work in Philadelphia, where he remained until 1888. The Philadelphia Church Choral Union was under the management of representatives of the different denominations, Mr. W. H. Wanamaker acting as president, Robert C. Ogden, vice-president, Rev. J. R. Miller, D. D., secretary and Dr. C. R. Blackall, treasurer. Its entire membership numbered over 5,000.

Mr. D. L. Moody was then preparing to begin instruction in his Bible Institute in Chicago, and engaged Mr. McGranahan to take charge of the musical department, where he began in 1889 and continued until 1894. Returning to Philadelphia he reorganized the Church Choral Union, and in addition to that work did private voice teaching, directed a choir and a male chorus at the Sunday afternoon meetings of the Central Y. M. C. A. Two notable occasions in this city was the directing of the music for the centennial celebration of the Presbyterian church, held in the Academy of Music, when in an afternoon meeting a choir of 1,200 sang, and in the evening an adult choir of 1,000, which, in connection with the congregation of about 4,000, united in a service of song. The other occasion was the Diamond Jubilee of the American Sunday-School Union, when a chorus of 1,000 sang "Gloria" by Mozart, and other strong choral selections, and led the singing of the great congregation.

At the close of this season Professor McGranahan suffered a severe nervous collapse and was unable to resume active work for nearly two years. He then took up work in Pittsburgh, doing class and private teaching, with choir work. Although a member of the Presbyterian church, he was engaged as musical instructor in the United Presbyterian Theological Seminary, and has edited several anthem books for the Publication Board of that church.

He has edited, in whole or in connection with others,

eight music books, including " Anthem Diadem," pub-
lished by The Biglow & Main Co.; "The Choral Class
Book," Theodore Presser ; "The Juvenile Class and Con-
cert," The John Church Company, and "Select Anthems,
Nos. 1, 2, 3 and 4." He has given some attention to
Summer Assembly work : directing the music at the Sea
Side Assembly, Avon-By-the-Sea, N. J., three seasons,
and at the Grove City (Pa.) Bible School five seasons.

He now resides at Jamestown, Pa., with his wife and
son, and is engaged in compiling and publishing music
books in Pittsburgh, but gives some time to directing
music in conventions and evangelistic meetings.

J. H. HALL.

LVI

J. H. Hall

THE subject of this sketch and author of this book, Jacob Henry Hall, was born January 2, 1855, near Harrisonburg, Rockingham County, Va. This is the most beautiful section of the Old Dominion, the great Shenandoah Valley of Virginia. He is a son of George G. and Elizabeth (Thomas) Hall. His father, being a farmer, brought up his son in the same vocation, and he served his time faithfully until he became of age. His parents and their entire family were quite musical. On his father's side his ancestry are English and Scotch, and on his mother's side German. The boy was always fond of helping his mother, and was her gardener as long as he remained at home.

He was passionately fond of music from childhood and his father sent him to the singing schools taught by Prof. Timothy Funk and others, where he learned to read music by note when but a small boy. During the winter months he attended literary school.

When a child a lady presented him with a mouth-organ and the music (if it could be called music) which he made always seemed to have more charm for himself than for any other member of the household. Later on by his industry he made money enough trapping quails to purchase a German accordeon, which he

soon learned to play one part while he would sing another, and this was to the delight of all.   Still later an
elder brother and himself purchased an organ.   In a
few months, and without the aid of a teacher, he learned
to play hymn-tunes, gospel songs, anthems, etc.

He always seemed to possess a rare determination to
succeed in learning the "divine art," and the real
dream of his boyhood was to become a musician and
teacher.   While working on the farm he would spend
the evenings and rainy days reading, singing and
studying theoretical works, preparing for his life-work.
When eighteen years of age he called on Prof. H. T.
Wartman, the most prominent musician at that time in
Harrisonburg, for advice concerning the study of music.
Their little conference was a pleasant one, and the professor presented the young aspirant with a copy of the
"Keystone Collection," by A. N. Johnson, a large
book which contained nearly one hundred pages of
Rudiments, Voice, Discipline, etc.   He soon mastered its
contents.   Professor Wartman invited him to attend his
classes in Harrisonburg and other places, which he did
with much profit.   The young man also studied theory,
harmony and composition with him, and he became his
favorite pupil, and assisted him in his classes.

In 1877 he attended a Normal Music School at New
Market, Va., conducted by Profs. B. C. Unseld and
P. J. Merges.   Here he got a clearer conception than
ever before what music teaching really meant.   He
was perfectly delighted with the methods.   At the
close of this school he entered into a partnership with
Professor Wartman in conducting singing schools and
conventions, in which they were eminently successful.
After two years of this pleasant association, Professor

Wartman moved to Florida; thus the partnership was dissolved.

In 1879 he attended another normal conducted by Professors Unseld and Merges. Mr. Hall was now able to do splendid work in the field of song and by his industry and enthusiasm he steadily gained prestige as a teacher.

He now decided to obey that Bible injunction that says, " It is not good that the man should be alone." So on January 23, 1883, he was married to Miss Elizabeth Frances Bowman, daughter of Rev. Joseph and Sarah (Flory) Bowman, a lady that has ever since been a helpmate truly and indeed, and who has ever encouraged Mr. Hall in his musical work. They reside in Dayton, Va., where they have a pleasant home. Their only child, Charles Ernest Hall, is a highly accomplished musician.

In 1885 he published a small collection of music, entitled, " Hall's Songs of Home."

In 1888 he attended another normal conducted by Professors Unseld and Merges.

The Ruebush-Kieffer Company now solicited the services of Mr. Hall to help make a class book. " The Star of Bethlehem " was the result of this effort. He wrote the Rudiments and arranged the book into Departments. It was a great success.

In 1890 he attended Dana's Musical Institute, Warren, Ohio. Here he made a fine record. He went out from this school with renewed energy into his normal work. In 1891 he invented " Hall's Music Chart," the greatest chart of its class. The late Professor Kieffer said, " ' Hall's Music Chart ' is the most comprehensive and complete chart in the world." In the same year

" Practical Voice Culture " was brought out. Also in the same year he attended a normal conducted by Dr. Geo. F. Root and Prof. F. W. Root, at Silver Lake, N. Y., and Dr. H. R. Palmer's School of Music, at Chautauqua, N. Y. These schools opened up a new musical world to him.

In 1892 " Fountain of Praise " was issued. In the same year he became a member of The Ruebush-Kieffer Company, and was chosen to assist Prof. A. S. Kieffer in editing the *Musical Million*, and he served in that capacity doing editorial work for seventeen years. Also in said same year he attended another session of Dr. Root's normal.

In 1893 " The Messenger of Song " was issued. In 1894 " Crowning Day, No. 1 " was issued. In the same year he attended the Philadelphia Summer School of Music, conducted by such eminent teachers and lecturers as Drs. Wm. Mason, W. S. B. Mathews, H. A. Clarke, and H. G. Hanchett, Profs. F. W. Root, W. H. Sherwood, L. C. Elson, C. W. Landon, J. C. Fillmore and others. Also in the same year he studied harmony with Dr. H. S. Perkins in The National College of Music, Chicago, and at the same time studied voice with Profs. D. A. Clippinger and C. B. Shaw.

In 1895 " Choir Anthems " and " The Vocal Gem " were published ; 1896, " Crowning Day, No. 2 " ; 1897, " The Normal Banner " and " Practical Harmony and Composition " ; 1898, " Crowning Day, No. 3 " ; 1899, " Sacred Hymnal " ; 1900, " Crowning Day, No. 4 " ; 1901, " Male Quartets " ; 1902, " Crowning Day, No. 5 " ; 1903, " Chorus and Choir " ; 1904, " Crowning Day, No. 6," and " Practical Music Reader " ;

1905, "Golden Thoughts and Memoirs"; 1906, "Sunlight of Praise"; 1907, "Male Quartets, No. 2"; 1908, "Crowning Day, Nos. 1–6," combined. This book contains only the *cream* of this famous series of gospel song books, and is by far the best gospel song book that has yet been published by The Ruebush-Kieffer Company. 1909, "Life and Light"; 1910, "Temperance Songs"; 1911, "Spirit of Praise," with Profs. C. C. Case and Wm. J. Kirkpatrick, associates; in 1912, "Hall's Quartettes for Men," published by D. W. Crist, Moultrie, Ohio. This is his finest quartette book. In 1913 "Sacred Melodies" was issued. The above is a partial list of Mr. Hall's more important works to date, and are all with the above exception published by The Ruebush-Kieffer Company, Dayton, Va. Some of his most popular gospel songs are: "Hurry and Tell Him," "The Gospel Invitation," "Open the Windows of Heaven," "Go and Tell Others the Story," "Jesus is Your Friend," "Helpers Are Needed," "We will Walk and Talk with Jesus," etc.

Through hard work, energy and close application, Mr. Hall has achieved success in his chosen profession. He worked his own way, and now often wonders how he surmounted the many obstacles which obstructed his path. He is principal of the National Normal School of Music, and has held sessions of this popular Institute in twenty different states, and has had as many as eight different states represented in a single session. It is an established fact that among the most practical musicians, authors and teachers, are those who have been trained and educated in first-class normals.

As a teacher and instructor, Professor Hall has few

equals. Clear, original and logical in his methods, firm in his convictions, yet kind, pleasant and unassuming in his manner, he immediately wins the respect and confidence of his pupils. His true manliness and integrity are above reproach. He is a member of the Brethren Church, and has conducted the music in a number of conferences and revivals; also directed the music in some of the late Rev. Sam Jones' great meetings. Long may he live and write many more beautiful gospel songs for the uplifting and betterment of humanity.

GEO. F. ROSCHE.

LVII

Geo. F. Rosche

THE subject of this sketch, George F. Rosche, was born August 18, 1855, near Navarre, Stark County, Ohio. His father being a farmer, the son spent his youthful days on the farm. When he was ten years of age he attended the first singing school that was organized in that section of the country, and he attended every term that was in walking distance. He also attended literary school. At the age of twelve his father purchased an organ and the boy began the study of music in earnest with Miss Christina Garver, who was an excellent teacher as well as a splendid pianist. At the age of fifteen he attended Dana's Musical Institute at Warren, Ohio, for the term of one year. He then began teaching piano and organ and followed this work by teaching singing schools, at all of which he was quite successful. During this time he was also studying harmony and composition with Rev. Corthauer, of Massillon, Ohio. When he was nineteen years of age he went to Stuttgart, Germany, and attended the Royal Conservatory of Music for two full years where he studied piano, pipe organ, harmony and composition and voice culture. Here he lived in a pure musical atmosphere. He listened to the great singers, pianists, and the best operas, and soon his taste for good music became very pronounced.

Mr. Rosche returned to America in 1876, and went

to Indianapolis, Ind., where he taught piano, etc., for three years. In 1879 he was called to the chair of music in the Seminary of the German Evangelical Synod of North America, located at Elmhurst, Ill. This position gave him an opportunity for developing his talent in theory and composition of music, which he taught in connection with piano, pipe organ and singing. He held this position for seven years and resigned in 1884 for the purpose of going into the piano and organ business and also music publishing, which was to some extent established during the seven years he spent at this seminary.

Mr. Rosche is now doing a handsome publishing business in Chicago, Ill. In 1897 *The Church Choir*, a monthly publication, was established which has been very successful and popular with choirs.

Some of his most popular gospel songs are: " Praise Him," " Have Faith In God," " He Keepeth Me Ever," " Resting in the Arms of Jesus," " Someday, Somewhere," etc.

He has edited and published a great many books, many of which are quite popular. These are mostly in the line of music for voices of women and voices of men; also anthem books for mixed voices in both the English and the German language. It is said that Mr. Rosche is the leading publisher of German church choir music in the United States.

He takes special pleasure in writing the music for Sunday-school cantatas and Sunday-school music in general. He has composed fifteen cantatas for the Sunday-school, all of which have met with success. Mr. Rosche seems to be especially gifted and successful in writing music for children.

In 1880 Mr. Rosche was married to Miss Ida Kate Weiser, of Indianapolis, Ind. They reside in Chicago, and have two sons and a daughter. The daughter is a graduate of the Chicago Art Institute. Mr. Rosche's musical contributions have put sunshine in many Sunday-schools, and both young and old have found much joy and profit in telling the gospel story in song.

CHAS. EDW. PRIOR.

LVIII

Chas. Edw. Prior

THE subject of this sketch, Charles Edward Prior, was born near Moosup, Conn., January 24, 1856, the son of Erastus L. and Sarah L. (Burleson) Prior. His interest in music dates from early childhood. When but three years old he sang "Rosalie, the Prairie Flower," and other popular songs, to the delight of the community. When he was about four years of age, the family moved to Jewett City, Conn., where he received a good common school education, and where his business career began. When fourteen years of age he became organist for the Congregational Church in Jewett City, and held the position for eight years, resigning to accept the position of chorister and organist for the Baptist Church, of which he is an active member. Here he at once formed a choir of young people, and they did excellent service in the church. He also organized an orchestra in the Sunday-school, which created much interest in that department.

While Mr. Prior has never devoted his time to convention work, his reputation as a leader has become wide-spread, and several Christian Endeavor Conventions in Connecticut have put the conducting of their song services entirely in his hands. He was elected musical director of the annual assemblies at Crescent Beach, held by the Connecticut Baptist Bible School

Union. He is a willing worker and the people appreciate his services. Mr. Prior has been an honorary member of the Worcester County Musical Association for many years, and takes an active interest in all of its affairs. It was while singing in the chorus at the festivals of this association that his love of oratorio music was kindled, and he became quite familiar with many of these grand compositions.

He is also familiar with the best gospel songs and church music in general. His first compositions were anthems for his choir, and were highly complimented. He then wrote a number of popular songs, of which more than fifty were published in sheet form. This list included sacred, sentimental, campaign, and temperance songs, some of them having a very flattering sale.

In 1883 his first song book, "Spicy Breezes," was published. He was assisted in the preparation of this book by one of his early pastors, Rev. C. W. Ray, D. D. In 1890 a new collection, "Sparkling and Bright," with J. H. Tenney as associate, was issued, and in 1892, in connection with W. A. Ogden, "Our Best Endeavor" was given to the public, and this book has met with general favor wherever used. Among Mr. Prior's most popular gospel songs we mention the following: "God is Our Refuge," "Are There Ten To-day?" "How Shall I Live?" "Linger Near Me, Blessed Saviour," "Loyal to Jesus," "The Lord is My Strength," "What Shall We Bring?" "The First Glad Song," "The Heavenly Land," "Beautiful Bethlehem," and "Stand and Speak." He has also contributed generously to many books of other authors.

Mr. Prior not only has musical talent, but he also has much business ability. Wherever he has been employed he has proved himself abundantly capable. It may be interesting to review his business positions and interests; also his church work. His first position was in the office of the Norwich & Worcester R. R. Co., in Norwich. In 1875 he became bookkeeper and pay-master for the Ashland Cotton Company, of Jewett City. He was elected secretary and treasurer of the Jewett City Savings Bank in 1883, and a few years later he became a member of the corporation and a director. In 1895 the position of assistant treasurer of the Security Company of Hartford was offered to Mr. Prior and accepted by him. In 1896 he was elected secretary and treasurer of the company and since November, 1904, has held the offices of vice-president and treasurer.

For six years he was president of the Hartford Baptist Union. He is also a director of the Hartford Y. M. C. A., and a member of the Connecticut Historical Society. Mr. Prior has been deeply interested in the Italian Baptist Mission in Hartford for a number of years, serving as pianist and as treasurer, and devoting much time and thought to the work. The success of this mission has been very pronounced, and Mr. Prior is acknowledged to have been an important factor in its prosperity.

Mr. Prior says that he owes much of his success in life to the influence of his sympathetic and helpful wife, who was Miss Mary Eleanor Campbell, of Jewett City. They reside in Hartford, Conn., and have one son, who is a fine singer and good business man.

May Mr. Prior live long and give to the world more of the true and beautiful in gospel song.

MISS E. E. HEWITT.

LIX

Miss E. E. Hewitt

ELIZA EDMUNDS HEWITT was born and educated in Philadelphia, Pa., and has always lived in that historic city. After her graduation from the normal school she began teaching, but this career was cut short by a serious spinal trouble, which rendered her a shut-in sufferer for a number of years. After a long period of pain and helplessness, health was gradually restored, but she has ever since been subject to physical limitations and occasional illnesses. While an invalid, she wrote a hymn for her pastor, Rev. Henry C. McCook, D. D., entitled " Winning Souls For Jesus." A copy of this hymn was placed in the corner-stone of the beautiful Tabernacle Church (Presbyterian), in West Philadelphia.

After this she wrote some motion songs for a friend to use in a primary Sunday-school. Some of her work came into the hands of the late Prof. J. R. Sweney, who wrote to her, asking for contributions. This was the beginning of her public work. Her labors were soon increased by the acquaintance of Prof. W. J. Kirkpatrick. For him she has written more extensively than for any other composer. Professor Sweney furnished music for some of her most popular hymns, such as " There is Sunshine In My Soul," " Will There Be Any Stars," and " More About Jesus." Professor

Kirkpatrick wrote to such favorites as "Stepping In the Light," "A Blessing in Prayer," "The Very Same Jesus," "Beautiful Robes," etc. Prof. J. H. Hall wrote music for several of Miss Hewitt's hymns; perhaps the most popular of these are: "Go and Tell Others the Story," "A Message From the King," and "Helpers are Needed." One of Miss Hewitt's hymns, "Not One Forgotten" (the original "Sparrow Song"), is especially dear to its author because of circumstances attending its composition, as well as its frequent use in hospital and other ministrations of love. It is always a great joy to hear of a blessing upon one's work, however humble that work may be, and Miss Hewitt is deeply grateful for the incidents that have come to her knowledge in connection with the use of her hymns. These incidents relate to every portion of our own beloved land, and also to the "uttermost parts of the earth." She has grouped these stories in a talk called "Around the World on the Wings of Song."

As time went on and strength increased, Miss Hewitt was able to take up the delightful work of Sunday-school teaching; she has a class of two hundred children. Her interest in this line led her to become a regular contributor to *Sunday-school Helps*, and to write poems and stories for children's papers.

She is a member of the Philadelphia Primary Union, often teaching the lesson there, and in other places.

Miss Hewitt is also interested, as should be every Christian, in missionary work, and frequently gives talks on missionary subjects in her own city and elsewhere.

The many pleasant friendships that have been formed with other writers, composers and publishers, are greatly appreciated by Miss Hewitt. No one feels more deeply than she the imperfections of her work, but such as it is, she lays at the Master's feet. He who multiplied the lad's loaves deigns to bless our humble offerings, and to use them in His service. To His name be the praise.

CHAS. H. GABRIEL.

LX

Charles H. Gabriel

WHEN, thirty years ago, the writer began a correspondence with a music writer whose chirography betrayed a youthful hand, he was quite certain that a brilliant future was before his correspondent. Some of the hymns which he furnished were so excellent that we were sure that a great hymn writer was about to win laurels, little suspecting that the hymn writer, excellent as he was, was to be overshadowed by the composer, and that the subject of this sketch was to win his laurels as a music writer rather than as a literary man. We remember with some amusement some of the advice we ventured to give our young friend, who, after all, was only a few years our junior, and who was, probably, fully as capable of giving as of receiving advice, even at that early day.

Charles Hutchison Gabriel was born in Iowa, August 18, 1856, and spent the first seventeen years of his life on a farm, building up the strong constitution which has enabled him to bear the strain which must necessarily fall upon the most copious popular composer of our time. At the age of seventeen he started out to hold singing classes and institutes throughout the Southern, Western, and Northern states, being thus brought into close contact with the people whose needs he so well understands how to meet. He later located in California, where he was recognized as the leading composer on the coast.

Mr. Gabriel has issued a large amount of music during the last thirty years, and we have not the space to give the long catalogue. He has been recognized as a leading writer of music for Sunday-schools, having issued *twenty-four* books for Sunday-schools and evangelistic meetings, his songs being found in almost every book that is issued. His first sacred song success, " Send the Light," is recognized as one of the best missionary songs extant, while scores of others, among which are: " Let the Sunshine In," " Calling the Prodigal," " The Way of the Cross Leads Home," etc., have large popularity. His " Glory Song " is no doubt the most popular song he ever wrote. The song may now be heard in many tongues and dialects. It has been translated into at least seventeen languages. It has appeared in print in leaflets, newspapers, magazines and books no less than 17,000,000 times. It is enjoyed by all classes and conditions from the street urchin to the nobility.

Mr. Gabriel has also been a prolific writer of anthems, having issued *fourteen* books in this particular line, besides many anthems prepared for other authors.

In no field, perhaps, has he done more brilliant work than in cantatas for children, of which he has written *seven*, both libretto and music. His " Dream of Fairyland " was exceedingly successful, and is still selling on its merits. His Christmas cantatas, of which he has written *thirty-eight*, have all been popular, tens of thousands of many of them having been sold. He has also prepared *eleven* sacred cantatas for adults ; *three* secular operettas and *one* sacred cantata—" Saul, King of Israel," which he considers his best work.

In his early days he was much interested in and a teacher of military bands, and has in print a goodly number of marches, waltzes, etc., for these organizations, beside instruction books for organ and piano, piano duets, solos, etc.

He is also the compiler of *three* books of music for female voices; *three* for male voices; *one* class book; *three* primary song books; *three* children's concert collections; more than *one hundred special day* programs, etc., etc.

Mr. Gabriel's music is nothing if not melodious. Even a comparatively commonplace theme under his pen receives some touch that gives it a perennial freshness, and while he rarely writes difficult or severe music, there is unbounded variety in it all. Having received little or no instruction, and being a self-made man, he has a style peculiarly his own. Copying no teacher or instructor, but following the natural bent of his genius, he is little hampered by purely scholastic rules of form, and hence is free to produce many effects and contrasts which other composers are apt to lose; yet his freedom deserves no censure, as it amply justifies itself in every case. He gives himself wholly to composition and his work is in constant demand by the various publishers of sacred music. Personally, Mr. Gabriel is a very genial and kindly-spirited man. His large success has not spoiled him, but seems rather to have added kindliness and helpfulness to his naturally generous disposition. He has no sense of rivalry with other composers and no inclination to emphasize their limitations or shortcomings. There is probably no composer in the land who has more friends among music writers, both famous and obscure, than Mr. Gabriel.

He resides in Chicago and is one of her honored citizens. May he live long and continue to give vent to his musical genius.

REV. JOHNSON OATMAN, JR.

LXI

Rev. Johnson Oatman, Jr.

THE subject of this sketch, Johnson Oatman, Jr., son of Johnson and Rachel Ann Oatman, was born near Medford, N. J., April 21, 1856. His father was an excellent singer, and it always delighted the son to sit by his side and hear him sing the songs of the church.

Outside of the usual time spent in the public schools, Mr. Oatman received his education at Herbert's Academy, Vincentown, N. J., and the New Jersey Collegiate Institute, Bordentown, N. J. At the age of nineteen he joined the M. E. Church, and a few years later he was granted a license to preach the Gospel, and still later he was regularly ordained by Bishop Merrill. However, Mr. Oatman only serves as a local preacher.

For many years he was engaged with his father in the mercantile business at Lumberton, N. J., under the firm name of Johnson Oatman & Son. Since the death of his father, he has for the past fifteen years been in the life insurance business, having charge of the business of one of the great companies in Mt. Holly, N. J., where he resides.

While Mr. Oatman does not fill any particular pulpit, yet he daily preaches to a larger congregation than the pastor of any church in the land. For through the medium of sacred song he preaches the Gospel to " all the world, and to every creature." " Let all the people praise the Lord."

355

Mr. Oatman is at the zenith of his years, and at this time he is one of the most prolific and popular gospel hymn writers in the world. He has written over three thousand hymns, and no gospel song book is considered as being complete unless it contains some of his hymns. He wrote his first song in 1892, which was brought before the people in 1893 by the late Prof. J. R. Sweney, and entitled " I Am Walking With My Saviour." From that time on Mr. Oatman has written and sent forth to bless the world an average of over two hundred songs each year. In a book published in Boston in the early part of his career as a song-writer, he made the following dedication :

> " Let others sing of rights or wrongs,
>   Sing anything that pleases ;
>   But while they're singing other songs,
>   I'll sing a song for Jesus."

In 1894 Professor Sweney wrote the music to one of Mr. Oatman's songs which at once gave him a place in the front ranks among American hymn writers. It is called " When Our Ships Come Sailing Home." It was sung at the great Ocean Grove, N. J., camp-meeting, and the people there went wild over it. The late Bishop C. C. McCabe sang it all over the United States. The chorus of the famous song is the following:

> " Oh, what singing, oh, what shouting, when our
>   ships come sailing home ;
>   They have stood the mighty tempests, they have
>   crossed the ocean's foam ;
>   They have passed o'er stormy billows, but they
>   now have gained the shore,
>   The anchor's cast, they're home at last, the voyage
>   is safely o'er."

About the same time Prof. W. J. Kirkpatrick introduced Mr. Oatman's " Deeper Yet." This song made
a way for itself into the hearts of all true worshippers.
There is a peculiar depth to it found in very few gospel songs.

" Deeper yet, deeper yet, into the crimson flood ;
Deeper yet, deeper yet, under the precious blood."

Then followed " Holy, Holy, Is What the Angels
Sing," brought out by Dr. H. L. Gilmour. This song
has only to be heard and its place is sure. But in 1895
appeared the song that has carried the name of Oatman to every clime and land on earth. The late Prof.
Geo. C. Hugg wrote the music to " No, Not One." It
went like wild-fire from the start. Within one year it
had been copied into thirty-five books and took a place
among the immortal songs of the religious world.
The late Bishop Isaac W. Joyce had the song translated into Chinese and Japanese. During the war in
South Africa the *Christian Herald* of New York had a
full-page picture of the Boer refugees on the border of
India engaged in worship, singing this popular song :

" Jesus knows all about our struggles,
He will guide till the day is done ;
There's not a friend like the lowly Jesus,
No, not one ! No, not one ! "

Many fine songs are only appropriate for certain
occasions, but " No, Not One " can be sung at any time,
place, or occasion. In 1897 the late Prof. J. H. Entwisle
introduced " Higher Ground." The music was written
by Mr. Chas. H. Gabriel, author of " The Glory Song."
This song at once took high rank among the holiness

people, and secured a lasting place in American hymnology. Nothing can bring forth more shouts at a camp-meeting of "Glory" and "Hallelujah" than the singing of "Higher Ground":

> "Lord, lift me up and let me stand,
> By faith, on heaven's table-land ;
> A higher plane than I have found,
> Lord, plant my feet on higher ground."

But it remained for Prof. E. O. Excell to bring out in 1897 what, in the opinion of most critics, is said to be Mr. Oatman's masterpiece. "Count Your Blessings," like "No, Not One," has gone all over the world. Like a beam of sunlight it has brightened up the dark places of earth. Perhaps no American hymn was ever received with such enthusiasm in England as "Count Your Blessings."

A London daily, in giving an account of a meeting presided over by Gypsy Smith, said, "Mr. Smith announced a hymn. 'Let us sing "Count Your Blessings."' Said he, 'Down in South London the men sing it, the boys whistle it, and the women rock their babies to sleep to the tune.'" During the great revival in Wales it was sung at every service, one of the leading dailies reporting the meetings, publishing in full, side by side, "The Glory Song" and "Count Your Blessings."

The foregoing are only a few of Mr. Oatman's songs that have won their way to the hearts of Christian people everywhere. "Take Off the Old Coat," "O Don't Stay Away," "The Blood Upon the Door," "The Same Old Way," "God's Three Hundred," "When the Fire Fell," "I Know He's Mine," "Almost

Home," and many others are among his best. He has constantly on hand more orders for songs than he can possibly fill. In a letter to Mr. Oatman in 1892 Professor Sweney said, " What we want and what we are looking for is something new." From that time on the song world has been getting from the pen of Rev. Johnson Oatman, Jr., something new. Withal, Brother Oatman is a firm believer in the good old doctrine of the Wesleyan theology.

On July 21, 1878, Mr. Oatman was united in marriage to Miss Wilhelmina Ried, of Lumberton, N. J. Mrs. Oatman was a most devout Christian lady, who walked by her husband's side and blessed his life until November 20, 1909, when the Lord called her to " Higher Ground."

Mr. Oatman has three children, a son and two daughters. The eldest daughter, Miriam E., is quite talented, and has written over three hundred hymns and is also a composer of music, having set music to several of her father's hymns. " How the Fire Fell " is perhaps the most widely known. Brother Oatman hopes to give to the world in the years to come the best songs of his life.

A. J. SHOWALTER.

LXII

A. J. Showalter

THE subject of this sketch, Anthony Johnson Showalter, was born at Cherry Grove, Rockingham County, Va., May 1, 1858, son of John A. and Susanna (Miller) Showalter. He received his education in the public schools. His first musical training was in the singing schools taught by his father. When but a lad he assisted his father in his singing classes.

In 1876 he attended his first normal music school at New Market, Va., conducted by Profs. B. C. Unseld and P. J. Merges. He then taught a number of singing schools, and later attended two more sessions of the same school. To still better prepare himself for the profession he attended a session of Dr. Geo. F. Root's normal at Erie, Pa., and Dr. H. R. Palmer's normal at Meadville, Pa. He now entered the music field with renewed energy and enthusiasm, teaching classes and conducting normals in various parts of the country.

In 1880 Mr. Showalter's first music book, "The Singing School Tribute," was published. In 1882 his "Harmony and Composition" was published, the first work of the kind by a Southern author. He has published two other works on the same subject since, and many song books. In 1884 he moved to Dalton,

Ga. Realizing the advantage of being able to publish his own productions, he established what has developed into The A. J. Showalter Company, one of the most thriving publishing houses in the South.

Mr. Showalter has been sole author, principal author and associate author of about sixty books, of which more than two million copies have been sold. Among his most successful books perhaps are: "Class, Choir and Congregation," "Work and Worship," "Glad Evangel," "Perennial Songs," "Rudiments," "Complete Rudiments," "Song Land Messenger," "Revival Choir," "Highway to Heaven," "Our Thankful Songs," "Singing for Joy," "Hymns of Glory," "Showalter's Gospel Songs, No. 3," "Sweetest Praise," "Day Dawn Songs," "Onward Songs," and "Revival Glory."

Among his many gospel songs none are more popular than "Leaning on the Everlasting Arms." This song has been published in many books, and sung wherever the story of Jesus has been told.

Mr. Showalter has edited *The Music Teacher*, now *The Music Teacher and Home Magazine*, for twenty-five years. He has held sessions of his Southern Normal Musical Institute in about a dozen different states and many teachers of the South and Southwest have attended this school.

In 1895 he availed himself of the opportunity to go to Europe with an excursion party, which proved to be both pleasant and profitable to him.

In 1905 Professor Showalter directed the "all day singing," a feature of the State Fair held at Atlanta, Ga. A chorus of several hundred voices joined in rendering a number of the good old gospel songs.

While writing and teaching music might be called

the life-work of Professor Showalter, he is also quite a successful business man with diversified interests. He is president of the A. J. Showalter Company, Dalton, Ga., and the Showalter–Patton Company, Dallas, Texas. He is also treasurer and manager of the Perry Brothers Music Company, Chattanooga, Tenn. Besides his musical interests he is vice-president of the Cherokee Lumber and Manufacturing Company of his home town, and a director in the Interstate Life and Accident Company of Chattanooga, Tenn., also a trustee of the Georgia Fruit Exchange, of Atlanta, Ga.

He finds recreation in spending some time in looking after his farm and extensive peach orchards near Dalton.

In 1881 Mr. Showalter was married to Miss Callie Walser, of Texas. They reside in Dalton, Ga., and have seven children, some of whom are splendid musicians. He is an active member in the Presbyterian church, also choir leader in his home church.

Professor Showalter has made the most of his opportunities, and success has crowned his efforts. " There is no excellence without great labor," and his work shows for itself that he has been a busy man. May he continue to render service in sacred song that will help some burdened soul to " Lean on the Everlasting Arms."

NOTE.—Since the above sketch of Mr. Showalter was written, there have been some very radical changes in both his business and family relations.

G. B. HOLSINGER.

LXIII

Geo. B. Holsinger

MANY of our greatest and grandest men in the various vocations of life have been reared on the farm—men of thought, character, honor and high ideals. Thank God for the noble band of farmer boys, who have been instrumental in helping to further the cause of putting humanity on a higher plane of usefulness. The subject of this sketch was one of those noble farmer boys, whose early years were spent on his father's farm. Geo. B. Holsinger was born May 10, 1857, in Bedford County, Pa.,—died November 22, 1908, in Astoria, Ill.

Our beloved brother was fond of music from childhood and at an early age attended singing schools taught by Prof. B. H. Everett. His first musical instrument was a German accordeon, with which he spent many pleasant hours. Then his father bought an organ, which gave much additional joy to the young lad, who was then seventeen years of age. Every spare moment—morning, noon and evening—was spent at the organ. He practiced so diligently (and without the aid of a teacher) that he learned to play any Sunday-school song, hymn-tune, or anthem. In 1876 a severe accident disabled him for farm work and he was sent to a normal school for public school teachers. Afterwards he taught school for some years. During this time he conducted singing schools at many places in the county, and later on would blush at the thought of the kind of work that he must have done. A little incident worth mentioning threw him into the field of musical labor. In failing to prepare and to perform satisfactorily a duty in a literary society, it was suggested that he redeem himself by singing a song instead, which was so well received that then and there he resolved to make music his life-work. In a few weeks he was on his way to Dayton, Va., to attend a musical normal to be taught by Prof. A. S. Kieffer and others. This was in 1881, and the same school was attended again the next year, taking the first prize in musical composition both years.

In 1882, at the establishing of the Bridgewater College at Bridgewater, Va., he was called to take charge of the musical department, which position he held for sixteen years. In 1888 he attended one of the most profitable normals of his educational course. It was held by Profs. B. C. Unseld and P. J. Merges. He also attended normals conducted by Dr. Geo. F. Root and Prof. F. W. Root, W. H. Pontius and J. M. Dungan, Dr. H. R. Palmer, and the Philadelphia Summer School of Music, conducted by such renowned teachers as W. S. B. Mathews, Wm. Mason, F. W. Root, J. C. Fillmore, H. A. Clarke, W. H. Sherwood, C. W. Landon, and others. In 1894 and 1895, during the month of August, were held sessions of the Bridgewater Summer Music School, with Professor Unseld as principal and Professor Holsinger taking the department of piano, organ and harmony.

In 1898 he was selected as musical editor of the Brethren Publishing House, Elgin, Ill., and resigned his position at the college to accept it. His new duties required a considerable portion of his time in the West, but he continued to reside in Bridgewater. Professor Holsinger was a good composer, an excellent teacher, and a sweet singer. He edited or assisted in editing not less than ten music books. Some of his most popular songs are, " Gathered Home," " At the Saviour's Right Hand," and " Steer Straight for Me, Father." The latter, with a dozen others, are published in sheet form.

In 1894 he was united in marriage with Miss Sallie A. Kagey of Bridgewater, a devoted Christian woman of fine literary ability. Their only living child is Clyde K. Holsinger. Brother Holsinger was a model Christian, a devoted member of the Church of the Brethren. He left home October 5, 1908 for a teaching tour and while conducting a school in Astoria, Ill., he contracted a cold which quickly developed into pneumonia. Tuesday evening, November 17th, he met his class for the last time, and on Sunday following, November 22d, he breathed his last. His body was brought back home for burial and was interred on Thanksgiving Day. In his death a good and valuable man is gone, but our loss is his eternal gain. We shall cherish his memory.

MRS. CARRIE B. ADAMS.

LXIV

Mrs. Carrie B. Adams

ONE of the most prolific and popular composers of sacred music is the subject of this sketch. Mrs. Adams is a favorite writer among choirs, and the natural melodic flow and harmonic treatment which she puts into her music greatly appeals to them.

Mrs. Carrie B. (Wilson) Adams was born in Oxford, Ohio, July 28, 1859. Her father, Mr. David Wilson, was author of a number of songs and books, also a singing teacher of note in his day, and her mother was quite musically inclined. This naturally made an attractive home and was the centre of a circle of friends who loved to sing. Mrs. Adams was early associated with her father and his close friends, Dr. Geo. F. Root, Dr. L. O. Emerson, Dr. H. R. Palmer and others, in musical conventions and institutes, first taking her place in the chorus with the altos at the age of seven in a convention held at Millville, Ohio, under the direction of Dr. H. R. Palmer. She became familiar with the choral works of the great masters, and her best work as director and composer has been done along this line. She has been a brilliant pianist and accompanist from her girlhood days. Her preference for the organ has been a source of inspiration in her chosen work—that of writing music for the average church choir, in which she has made a great success.

Her experience with her father in elementary and

advanced class work, in children's and harmony classes, her years of musical participation in solo work and in accompanying, in the organization and leadership, not only of choirs, but also of great choral organizations, her close touch with singers of elementary grade, as well as those of great skill and reputation, have given her a breadth of musical thought and practical power of adaptation that constantly enrich her work of composition.

Miss Carrie B. Wilson became Mrs. Allyn G. Adams in 1880, and soon after located in Terre Haute, Ind., where her husband was and is a leading bass singer and interested in large commercial enterprises. Mrs. Adams soon became a leading figure in the musical life of that enterprising city, and has been actively identified with the Choral Club, Treble Clef Club, Rose Polytechnic Glee Club, First Congregational Church and Central Christian Church choirs, as director, chorister and organist. From 1887 to 1895 she occupied the chair of music in the Indiana State Normal School.

For many years Mrs. Adams was associated with Prof. W. T. Giffe in institute work, also composed anthems for his *Choir Music Journal.* She has also given much attention to music in the public schools.

In 1901 " The Messiah " was given under her direction by a chorus of one hundred and fifty voices, with soloists of recognized ability. She has directed a number of other great and important works.

Her first anthem was published in 1876. Among her best known publications are four anthem books— " Anthem Annual, Nos. 1 and 2," and " Royal Anthems, Nos. 1 and 2 " ; " Music for Common Schools " ; two sacred cantatas, "Redeemer and King " and "Easter

Praise "; an operetta for church and school use, "The National Flower "; a group of Shakespeare songs from " As You Like it," and a large number of anthems, male choruses, ladies' quartets and miscellaneous pieces in octavo form. "Remember Now Thy Creator " is a favorite with high school choruses as well as choirs. An arrangement of " 'Tis Midnight Hour," "Merry Girls Are We " and " The Streamlet's Song," are popular with ladies' quartets or choruses. A number of her sacred solos and songs are beautiful.

Mrs. Adams writes regularly for *The Choir Herald*, published by Mr. E. S. Lorenz. She has almost completed the manuscript for a Christmas cantata and compiled an anthem book this season, in addition to much musical work of a local character. She is a busy writer, and her music is popular and is doing great good in the world. May Mrs. Adams live long and continue her excellent musical work.

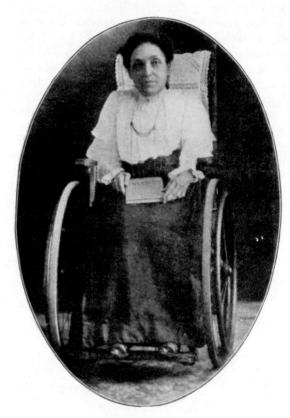

MISS JENNIE WILSON.

LXV

Miss Jennie Wilson

MANY of the beautiful soul-stirring gospel hymns that have cheered, encouraged, and blessed a great multitude of hearts have been written by Miss Jennie Wilson, of South Whitley, Ind.

It is a blessed privilege and deserving of honor to tell the "old, old story" in verse and song, and thus inspire the armies of salvation to conquer the world for Jesus. Miss Wilson's work is of unusual interest, not only by its extent and quality, but for the extraordinary conditions under which it has been produced. She is an invalid, having been lame from childhood, yet her whole life has been a bright example of talent, which she has used in the Master's service.

For a number of years the name of Jennie Wilson has been a familiar one among singers and song writers as a composer of gospel hymns. Yet there are but few who know that she is the occupant of an invalid's wheel-chair. She was born near South Whitley, on the farm where she now resides in the family of her sister, Mrs. J. Ulrey. Her father died in her infancy. When she was about four years old, an attack of spinal trouble resulted in rendering her an invalid.

Not being able to attend school, she studied at home, read much and received some musical instruction. A natural love for music and poetry early led her to verse writing. Her first poems appeared in a local paper.

Later, through the influence of Rev. J. D. Coverstone, she sent hymns to a publication in Dayton, Ohio. These attracted the attention of music writers, by whom she was invited to write hymns to be set to music.

Miss Wilson's first hymn was entitled, "All the Way," and, not knowing of its publication, she was pleasantly surprised when it was found in new song books purchased by a Sunday-school in her neighborhood. Miss Jennie Wilson has written *twenty-two hundred* poems. Among the most useful and popular of these the following may be mentioned : " Beautiful City of Peace," " Precious Golden Grain," "Jesus is Calling the Children," etc., set to music by Wm. J. Kirkpatrick. We also mention, " There Will be Light at the River," " Is it Well with Your Soul ? " " Listen to the Spirit's Call," "Go Forth to the Battlefield," " I've No Other Place to Go," " Christ is Calling You To-night," and " Mercy's Door is Always Open." Miss Wilson has been assured that several of these hymns have been blessed to the conversion of many souls. "Answer 'Yes' to the Spirit," "In the Light of Eternity," and " Hold the Lamp of Life Aloft," set to music by E. S. Lorenz, are also quite popular.

Miss Wilson shows no trace of invalidism in her literary work. One of her poems entitled, " A Memory Picture," is an exception. It refers to scenery near the old home, and alludes to memories of the time when she could walk. During the summer season she attends the Bible conferences at Winona Lake, Ind., and other places, which affords her great spiritual enjoyment.

Her mother died in 1902. Her grave is marked by a monument bearing the following verse written by

the invalid daughter to whom she had given years of
devoted care:

> " After her long life journey
> Cometh death's dreamless sleep;
> Over her rest may angels
> Ever a fond watch keep."

Miss Wilson is a fine exemplification of the power of
divine grace, having passed through the ordeal of suffering and come out of it a spiritualized and refined
nature, and with a talent which has become a blessing.
She is a small woman, only five feet in height, and seems
still smaller in her chair. But her sunny nature and
gentle, intellectual face would win friends anywhere.

She was baptized in 1881, being carried on a chair
into a beautiful tree-shaded stream, and, in her words:
"It gave me much joy to thus confess my dear Saviour." Miss Wilson has tuned her heart to the strains
of praise and thanksgiving and Christian cheer and invitation, has all unconsciously been made the instrument
to win many precious souls from sin to righteousness.
In one of her own verses, she voices the longing for
that larger freedom which will be hers some day:

> " But in the land more fair than day,
> From bondage free, I hope to stray
> By life's pellucid river,
> The sunny hills of heaven climb,
> And through God's balmy summertime,
> Range joyously forever."

NOTE.—Soon after the above sketch was written, Miss Wilson
passed to the " *Great Beyond.*" Her death occurred September 3,
1913, in her fifty-sixth year.

Her sweet and devoted Christian life, and her many beautiful
hymns, should erect to her memory an enduring monument.

H. N. LINCOLN.

LXVI

H. N. Lincoln

THE subject of this sketch, Horace Neely Lincoln, was born May 14, 1859, in Mexico, Audrain County, Mo., where his childhood to the age of seven was spent with the family of his parents, Mr. James and Mrs. Emaline Lincoln. In the fall of 1866 they all "embarked" in covered wagons for Texas, in company with a large caravan of immigrants (there being no such convenience as railroad travel in that country at this time). Only those who have had similar experience can appreciate the old-fashioned overland trip.

In due course of time the Lincoln family were introduced to the savage wilds of Texas. At the age of ten years, Horace attended his first singing school, taught by Mr. James M. Jolley, of Mississippi. He showed evidences of musical talent and soon had the distinction of being the boy singer of the country for miles around. He attended other singing schools taught by Mr. J. M. Deavors, and still later was a real earnest student of Mr. L. B. Shook, who had studied with Mr. P. P. Bliss. In 1880 he taught his first singing class in his old neighborhood schoolhouse. Later in the year he attended his first normal music school, taught at Mountain Home, Bell County (the present site of Holland). This normal was conducted by Prof. L. B. Shook and Prof. John McPherson of Illinois.

These days were the beginning of the musical era of the Southwest. In rapid succession after this school, Mr. Lincoln taught many singing schools in all parts of Texas, and soon had a number of bright students in the new but fertile musical field and the cause of sacred song waxed strong. In 1885 appeared Mr. Lincoln's first song book entitled "Gospel Carols." Several thousand copies of this book were sold, but the first real successful book of which he was author was "Songland Messenger," which sold by the tens of thousands. But the most successful of all books in the point of circulation of which he is author is "Songland Melodies," which has reached the sale of several hundred thousand copies. He is author of more than a dozen very successful books.

On September 4, 1887, Mr. Lincoln was wedded to Miss Etta Lee Thurmand, a lady who has helped and encouraged him all along in his work.

Mr. Lincoln may be easily termed the pioneer teacher, singer and author of any note in the Southwest, but now this great section is literally swarming with singing school teachers and evangelistic singers.

He graduated in 1898 under Dr. H. S. Perkins in the Chicago National College of Music. In 1906 he took a post-graduate course under the late Dr. H. R. Palmer, of New York City.

Mr. Lincoln has accomplished a vast amount of work in laying a foundation for musical development in the great state of Texas. He has written a great number of both sacred and secular songs; perhaps among his most useful and popular sacred songs are: "The Lost Soul's Lament," "Satan's Lullaby," "The Beacon Light," "Let Jesus Reign," "Meet Me Over

There," " When the Light Breaks Through," and "The Music of His Voice." He has written a great many other useful gospel songs, many of which are especially good as solos or quartets.

Mr. Lincoln has a pleasant home in Dallas, Texas, where he resides with his interesting family. He is president of the Songland Music Company, and of The World's Normal Music College, both of which are incorporated. He is yet in the prime of his usefulness and much more may be expected from him. He is a member of the First Baptist Church of Dallas, of which Geo. W. Truett is the pastor. Let the good work go on; "for it is good to sing praises unto our God; for it is pleasant; and praise is comely."

C. D. TILLMAN.

LXVII

Charlie D. Tillman

THE subject of this sketch, Charlie D. Tillman, was born March 20, 1861, at Tallassee, Ala. His parents were consecrated Christians, and travelled a great deal holding evangelistic meetings. Charlie had but few advantages for either a literary or musical education. He was extremely fond of music from childhood, and by his study and practice he has made quite a success in the music business. When but a mere lad he led the music in the meetings which his parents held in the rural districts of North Carolina, but he soon became tired of the work and gave it up. Then after two years of house and sign painting, giving concerts, and putting in a little time on one of the Wizard Oil Carriages as singer of comic songs and second tenor in a male quartet, he secured a position as travelling salesman for a music house in Raleigh, N. C. He proved to be a good salesman, and on one occasion he made a sale to a man whose dwelling was not worth as much as the organ which he sold him. After following this work for some time, he again joined his parents in the evangelistic work.

By this time he could play his own accompaniments and do solo singing which was highly complimented and greatly encouraged him in the work. Mr. Tillman now felt and realized the power of gospel song as he had never realized it before. With renewed zeal and spiritual interest he fully resolved to spend his life in the evangelistic field in both sermon and song. He now realized that he needed a song book for revivals, and his first attempt in this line was a small booklet of thirty-two pages in character notes. He soon added to this thirty-two pages more. He then began editing and publishing his series of revival song books, the sale of which has now gone considerably over a million copies. In 1908 he brought out "Sunday-School and Revival," a book whose sales are already nearing the two hundred and fifty thousand mark. Mr. Tillman has edited a dozen or more books. Among his most popular and widely known gospel songs are the following: "My Mother's Bible," "Life's Railway to Heaven," "Save One Soul for Jesus," "Ready for Service," "The Spirit is Calling," and "Old Time Power."

Mr. Tillman married Miss Annie Killingsworth, a lady who has ever been a faithful helpmate. They reside in Atlanta, Ga., where they have a pleasant home and an interesting family. Mr. Tillman does a thriving publishing business in connection with his evangelistic work.

Long may he live and continue to help spread the name of Jesus in the world in sermon and song.

MISS IDA L. REED.

LXVIII

Miss Ida L. Reed

IDA L. REED was born November 30, 1865, near Philippi, Barbour County, W. Va. She had but few educational advantages in childhood, but she was quite studious, and would spend many of her play hours reading, for she loved it more than play. Fortunately for her, she had access to many papers, journals and magazines, which she read with great pleasure and profit. When she was seventeen years of age, she passed her first examination and received a first-grade certificate. She then taught school for several years, but on account of sickness she had to finally give up school-teaching. Later she attended school for a time at Lebanon, Ohio.

But He who directs our ways had a more important work than teaching school for Miss Reed, namely, that of writing gospel poems, for the Gospel in song is one of the helps in evangelizing the world. So she fully resigned and consecrated herself to the Master's work.

She began writing hymns in her twentieth year, and has composed some of the most helpful hymns that are to be found in the gospel song books of the present day, and seem to continue to grow in popularity. Her father died in 1892; this necessitated her to look after the farm as well as to care for her mother, which she did faithfully and loyally until the death of her mother in 1906.

During all these years of toil she would compose hymns, recitations, exercises for Sunday-schools, etc., while her hands were busy with other tasks.

Miss Reed is a very prolific composer; with all the burdens and cares of her life, besides ill health, she has written more than two thousand hymns, cantatas, etc., etc., which have been widely published in the books used by different denominations. Her hymns that have become most popular are: "I Belong to the King," "I Cannot Drift Beyond Thy Love," "Somebody Is Praying for You," "Speak O Lord," "The Father's Love," "Blessed Hiding," "He Knoweth Thy Grief," and many others have been used to His glory.

She loves her work and her highest aim and deepest heart longing, her one constant prayer, is that she may be able to make her work a power for good, strong enough to win souls to God from their wanderings and help them to come into the full light of His peace and love.

After the death of her mother she moved to her home town, Philippi, where she now resides. During these years she has lived by herself, practically shut in from the world, owing to frail health. Miss Reed is a most devoted and consecrated Christian lady, patient, kind and always thankful for the kindnesses shown her by her friends. She says, "He who has been so faithful through all my yesterdays will not fail me through my to-morrows." May Miss Reed be permitted to write many more sweet inspiring gospel poems for the betterment of mankind.

J. LINCOLN HALL.

LXIX

J. Lincoln Hall

THE subject of this sketch, Joseph Lincoln Hall, was born in Philadelphia, November 4, 1866. His parents, Joseph M. and Barbara Hall, were musicians of considerable merit, and from them the son inherited his musical talent and was very fond of music. He had the usual routine of public school life in his youthful days. At the age of nineteen years he was appointed choir master of a choir of over one hundred members, and he led this choir successfully for over ten years.

Mr. Hall was graduated in music with high honors from the University of Pennsylvania, studying music under Dr. H. A. Clarke. He studied harmony, counterpoint, fugue and orchestration; and for a graduating thesis composed a Mass, in D, orchestrated for the full orchestra.

He is also an alumnus of Harriman University, from which university he received the degree of Mus. Doc. He is truly an educated musician.

Mr. Hall has been director of music at a number of the great camp-meetings of which I mention the following: Chester Heights, Pa., Rawlinsville, Pa., Waterloo, Ohio, and Landisville, Pa. He has led the large chorus at Pitman Grove and is conductor of music at Gainesville Bible Conference, Gainesville, Fla. He has conducted large choruses in various parts of the country and his services are in great demand for large choruses and congregations throughout the country. Mr. Hall was selected to lead the singing at Ocean Grove campmeeting for the season of 1910.

But it is with J. Lincoln Hall as a composer that we have to deal mostly in this sketch. Mr. Hall is many-sided in his writing and has written everything in the music line from an oratorio in the classic style to a simple gospel song. Some of his most popular compositions are: "The Shepherd King," an oratorio; "From Cross to Crown," a cantata; and "Prophecy and Fulfillment," a cantata. He has written many anthems for the choir that have had immense sales; such as, "As the Hart," "Hail King of Glory," "Wake, O Judean Land," and over fifty other popular anthems that are in print.

Mr. Hall has written a great many gospel and Sunday-school songs; among the most popular of these are: "Does Jesus Care," "Some of These Days," "Victory," "Looking Beyond," "The Banner of the King," "Working for Jesus," etc. He has also edited a great many gospel song books, some of which have reached an enormous sale. "Voice of Praise," "Voice of Praise, No. 2," "Service of Praise," "Boundless Love," and the "New Songs of the Gospel" series have been among the most successful of these books. His services for various occasions have been in great demand for the past fifteen years.

Mr. Hall does a thriving publishing business in Philadelphia, under the firm name of Hall–Mack Company.

In 1896 Mr. Hall married Miss Eva Withington, of Philadelphia, daughter of Thomas and Margaret Withington. They reside in Philadelphia.

Dr. Hall is still a young man and has before him many years of usefulness. As a writer, as a singer gifted with a beautiful tenor voice, as a theorist, as a teacher, and as an organist, he is in the front rank and is in great demand.

J. S. FEARIS.

LXX

J. S. Fearis

JOHN S. FEARIS was born in Richland, Iowa, February 5, 1867. His father was a successful singing school teacher, as well as a painter by trade. The son learned to read music in his father's classes when but a small boy. He was passionately fond of music and took lessons on the reed organ, and was soon able to play in Sunday-school and church. Later he took charge of the church choir, and also taught singing classes in the neighboring towns and country schoolhouses. In the summer season he would join his father in house painting. He studied and practiced music diligently at every opportunity, and soon was able to give lessons on the organ and in singing. He now fully decided to make music his life-work. When a mere boy his talent and inclination for musical composition were quite decided. His first song, a hymn-tune, was published when he was sixteen years of age.

He kept up his work of teaching and after a time joined two other men in conducting musical conventions in various parts of the country. This work was continued for several years, and success crowned their efforts. While in this work, Mr. Fearis did considerable writing, and Mr. Alfred Beirly, of Chicago, published an anthem for him in his *Choir Serial*. This was soon followed by other church music, and he finally accepted an offer made by Mr. Beirly and located in Chicago, where he has been a busy man ever since.

Mr. Fearis is an excellent composer of all styles of composition—gospel songs, anthems and secular songs. He is on the editorial staff of the *Choir Leader*, published by The Lorenz Publishing Company, of Dayton, Ohio.

He has also written a great deal of piano and organ music, especially teaching pieces, as he has a knack of making easy pieces sound well. Of late years he has studied harmony and composition under Adolph Weidig, which has developed a wide range in musical composition. Mr. Fearis is doing quite a publishing business in the line of octavo anthems, male quartets, ladies' quartets, and solos in sheet form.

He has written many beautiful gospel songs. Perhaps among his most popular are: " Beautiful Isle of Somewhere," " Songs in the Night," " The Promise Made to Mother," " Wherever He Leads Me I'll Go," and " Show Me the Way, My Shepherd."

While Mr. Fearis devotes much of his time to writing and publishing, yet he finds time to do some teaching and also conducts some of the choral societies of the city.

May health and strength be his for many years to come in the service of song, and may his work influence thousands to strive for that " Beautiful Isle of Somewhere."

W. E. M. HACKLEMAN.

LXXI

W. E. M. Hackleman

THE subject of this sketch has not only achieved success as a composer and publisher of gospel songs, but also as a leader and singer.

W. E. M. Hackleman was born February 28, 1868. He spent his youthful days tilling the soil of an Indiana farm. He attended the district and other schools, also singing schools. He made rapid progress in his musical studies, and at the age of seventeen began teaching singing classes and leading the singing in meetings, also sang solos. Later on he taught public school for four years.

To make a more thorough preparation for his life-work he studied in the Toronto Conservatory of Music, Toronto, Canada. He also studied under private teachers in New York City.

Since that time he has been busy composing, editing song books, and leading the music in State and National Conventions of the Christian Church. He has led the music in meetings in Boston, New York, Philadelphia, Pittsburgh, Cincinnati, Chicago, St. Louis, Des Moines, Louisville, Memphis, Washington, D. C., Indianapolis, and many other large centres. He led the music of communion service, Centennial Convention, Pittsburgh, in which 30,000 people joined in singing " as with one mighty voice."

In 1899 Mr. Hackleman married Miss Pearl Damie Conner, the accomplished daughter of Rev. A. W. Conner. They reside in Indianapolis, Ind.

Mr. Hackleman is president of the National Association of Church Musicians, and through this is lending a helping hand to many competent and worthy singers. He was secretary of the Indiana Missionary Society for five years, and for the past three years has been secretary of Bethany Assembly.

He is a member of the firm of Hackleman Music Company, Indianapolis, Ind., and is editor or co-editor of some twenty-five books, including " Gloria In Excelsis," a church hymnal. He considers this his best work. His song books cover the different departments of church work. His hymnological library is said to be one of the largest and best in the country. Hymnody is his hobby and upon that subject he is well-nigh an authority. Among his most useful gospel songs are: " Drifting Down," " Saved By Mother's Prayer," " This Way, Papa," " What Will You Do with Jesus ? " " Who Cares for a Soul ? " " The Wondrous Cross," etc.

Mr. Hackleman is doing excellent work for the good of .humanity. May he live long and write many more gospel songs that will cheer and encourage some heart to live on " higher ground."

GRANT C. TULLAR.

LXXII

Grant C. Tullar

GRANT COLFAX TULLAR was born in Bolton, Tolland County, Conn., August 5, 1869. His father had been incapacitated for active work through injuries received at the battle of Antietam. His mother died when he was two years old, leaving a family of nine children. On the day of her burial the family was scattered, never to be together as a family again. Grant had no settled home after that day till he had become a man and had one of his own, but he lived a few months or a few years in a place, having practically no educational advantages, no religious or home training, and at the age of ten began to earn his own way by working in a woolen mill. For the next few years he had a very checkered career, suffering the usual privations of the homeless, friendless waif.

After working a few months at the mill, he went to Hartford, Conn., where he secured a job as errand boy in a shoe store. This job he held for two and a half years, rising to the position of bookkeeper. He then accepted a position in a wholesale shoe-house in Boston, Mass., and after spending a few months in that city, he went to Waterbury, Conn. He was now nineteen years of age, and while attending a meeting, was led to Christ through the earnest consecrated effort of Mrs. H. F. Conrad, of that city, and with the new life

401

opened before him everything changed for the better, "old things passed away and behold all things became new." He felt that he had a call to religious work and at twenty years of age he entered Hackettstown Academy, New Jersey.

After two years of hard study he was compelled to give up the course on account of poor health. During these two years special talent was shown along gospel hymn lines, which was destined to be developed by practical work in the evangelistic field into which he was led during the succeeding years.

Mr. Tullar has preached the Gospel in sermon and in song in all parts of the United States and Canada, also in many other parts of the world. In 1893, in association with Mr. I. H. Meredith, formed the Tullar–Meredith Company, whose publications are now well known wherever gospel songs are sung. These gentlemen are also associated in evangelistic work.

In 1898 Mr. Tullar married Miss Anna Belle Woods, at Aledo, Ill.; they reside at East Orange, N. J.

Among the numerous songs which Mr. Tullar has given to the world in recent years probably the best known are: "Face to Face," "Nailed to the Cross," "Forward" and "He Did Not Die in Vain." The books which he. has been associated in editing are as follows: "Sermons in Song," "Sunday-School Hymns," "The Bible School Hymnal," "The Sacrifice of Praise," "Children's Praise," "Songs Sacred and Secular," a book for male voices, "The American Songster," "Hymns of Worship and Praise" and "Manly Songs for Christian Men." All the above works are published by the Tullar–Meredith Company, of New York City.

Mr. Tullar is doing good work in the Master's vine-yard, both preaching and singing the Gospel with telling effect. May he live long and continue to reap for Him who has invited the world to come unto Him and be saved.

I. H. MEREDITH.

LXXIII

I. H. Meredith

THE subject of this sketch, Isaac H. Meredith, was born at Norristown, Pa., March 21, 1872. His parents were both born in England and in early manhood his father played the violin and his mother sang in the choir. His father's reverent love of music he considers his greatest musical heritage, and the singing of old English carols by his father and mother to the accompaniment of the violin are among the most blessed memories of his early childhood. Before he was ten years of age he began taking organ lessons from a local teacher and these continued for several years. He sang alto in the church choir before he was twelve and at thirteen he was converted through the personal invitation of his brother, B. F. Meredith, now a Methodist clergyman. Almost immediately after his conversion he felt a definite call to the ministry of sacred song. He spoke little of this to any one but kept it as a treasure in his own heart, feeling assured that God would eventually lead him into the work if such was His will. Even in these early boyhood days he sang gospel songs with much tenderness and power. At twelve he became organist of the local Y. M. C. A., and played continuously for the association until his entrance into evangelistic work at the age of nineteen.

After his conversion he sang for a number of years

each Sunday morning to the prisoners at the county jail. In the summer of 1891 he went to Ocean Grove, N. J., to spend his vacation and while there met Prof. J. J. Lowe, who was then singing with Dr. Munhall, the well-known evangelist. Mr. Lowe invited him to play for him in the evening and while the service was proceeding asked him to sing a solo at the close of the sermon. This he did, singing Sankey's " When the Mists Have Rolled Away." This was so well received that it led to an arrangement with Rev. G. L. Barker, who was leading the Young People's meeting that year, to enter evangelistic work with him as his singer. This was towards the last of August, and early in September he began his first engagement at South River, N. J. Soon after his entrance into evangelistic work he began composing gospel songs and his early efforts were purchased by Sankey, Excell, Bilhorn and others. Finally he began to publish his own music, uniting with Mr. Grant C. Tullar, who was also in evangelistic work, and the Tullar–Meredith Company, New York and Chicago, is the outgrowth of this union.

Mr. Meredith has composed over a thousand songs, consisting principally of gospel songs and festival songs for the Sunday-school, also a number of anthems and cantatas. He is associated with Mr. Tullar in editing and publishing quite a number of popular gospel song books. He has held important church positions in New York as soloist and choir director.

Mr. Meredith has toured England with Torrey and Alexander in evangelistic meetings. He has directed the music in conventions throughout the country. The training and experience which he has had assures success in his chosen work.

" Thine to work as well as pray,
   Clearing thorny wrongs away ;
   Plucking up the weeds of sin,
   Letting heaven's warm sunshine in."

I. ALLAN SANKEY.

LXXIV

I. Allan Sankey

THE subject of this sketch, I. Allan Sankey, was born in Edinburgh, Scotland, August 30, 1874, son of Ira D. and Fanny V. Sankey. Allan's father was the greatest singing evangelist of his day. His pure life and sweet inspiring gospel songs should be an incentive for every young person to cultivate their musical powers for doing good in the world. The musical mantle of the great singer and musician seems to have fallen on his son Allan, and he has already achieved much success in the music business. His early education was received in the public schools. Later he entered Princeton University, and graduated from that institution in 1897. His special studies were civil engineering and architecture. He also took a pretty thorough course in music.

In 1898 Mr. Sankey had the honor bestowed upon him to become the president of the famous publishing house—The Biglow & Main Co., New York City.

In 1899 Mr. Sankey was married to Miss Frances Wann, of New York City. They reside in Brooklyn, N. Y.

Among his popular books we mention the following: "The Male Quartette," in connection with Mr. Geo. C. Stebbins; "Best Endeavor Hymns," joint editor with Mr. John R. Clements, and sole editor and compiler of "Hallowed Hymns, New and Old." Of this last named book nearly two hundred thousand copies were sold during the first fourteen months.

He has composed some very popular sacred songs. Perhaps the best known are : " Never Give Up, " Kept for Jesus," etc.

Besides Mr. Sankey's musical ability as editor and composer, he also has much business ability. Apart from the publishing house, he is vice-president of the Leeds and Catlin Phonograph Company, and is also a member of the Advisory Board of the Greenich Bank.

Mr. Sankey is yet a young man and much more may be expected of him. May the Lord bless his efforts in helping to advance the cause of sacred song in the world.

IRA B. WILSON.

LXXV

Ira B. Wilson

I
T is not given to many composers to make an impression on the general public so early and quickly as has Mr. Ira B. Wilson. The fertility of his musical suggestiveness, the clearness of his musical impressions and the sureness of his musical instinct have brought him to the very front in the course of a few years. He is by all odds the most promising young anthem and gospel song writer in his age and generation.

Ira B. Wilson was born September 6, 1880, in Bedford, Taylor County, Iowa, and came from a family which was known for miles around his home as a musical family. Almost all of his early instruction he received from an elder sister. He thus grew up in an atmosphere in which music played an important rôle as far as the intellectual life of the family was concerned. He learned to play on the violin and organ and had begun harmony before leaving home.

At the age of about twenty-two he went to Chicago to the Moody Bible Institute with a view to training himself for an evangelistic singer. While here he directed a number of choirs in various churches in Chicago. He studied harmony under Dr. D. B. Towner. He soon began works of composition and within a year his songs were being accepted by all the leading gospel song publishers in the country.

413

After leaving Chicago, Mr. Wilson became manager of the young people's work in the First Presbyterian Church at Oshkosh, Wisconsin. He continued successfully his work in composition, writing his first anthems while here. He also organized and led a very successful Sunday-school orchestra, which inspired him to a careful study of orchestration in order to supply the needed music. He has since that time made numerous orchestra arrangements and has been one of the editors and arrangers of a very successful collection of pieces for church orchestras.

Early in 1904, Mr. Wilson was called to assist in the editorial work of The Lorenz Publishing Company of Dayton, Ohio, which position he still occupies and is doing efficient service not only in composition, but in other lines of editorial work. His range of composition is very wide.

While writing a great amount of music for Sunday-schools, he is a regular contributor to the two monthly journals published by The Lorenz Publishing Company, *The Choir Leader* and *The Choir Herald*. He has prepared several successful choir cantatas, secular cantatas for Sunday-school, and has also written considerable organ music and quite a number of sacred solos. His chosen field—the one in which he feels most at home— is supplying music for the church and Sunday-school, but he has written some very successful secular choruses and solos.

One remarkable feature of Mr. Wilson's musical talent is its adaptability. He is quite as much at home in the writing of a primary song as in the composition of a full anthem. While his lighter music is very bright and gay at times, his more serious music is often full of tenderness and sentiment. With the growth that the coming years will undoubtedly bring him, there is no reason why he should not secure a very prominent place in the history of American church music.

ROBERT HARKNESS.

LXXVI

Robert Harkness

IN June, 1902, Dr. R. A. Torrey and Mr. Charles M. Alexander held a meeting in Bendigo, Australia. Here Mr. Alexander first met Mr. Robert Harkness, a brilliant young musical genius, who is the subject of this sketch.

Mr. Alexander at once recognized his superior musical gifts and engaged him as his pianist, a position he still holds. He also led him to Christ. Mr. Harkness made the decision to accept Christ as he rode along on his bicycle after a long talk with Mr. Alexander at a hotel in Bendigo.

Mr. Robert Harkness was born in Bendigo, Australia, March 2, 1877. He was reared in a Christian home, his father being a godly man, a local preacher and one of the most honored and respected men in Bendigo; his mother, one of those saintly women, commands the highest respect of all who know her.

Mr. Harkness is an accomplished musician, with several years of training and experience as a church organist and choir director. He wanted to compose music at an early age. His first published song appeared in 1896. He has since achieved international fame as a composer of gospel songs as well as a pianist. He has written some of the most popular hymns used by Mr. Alexander.

Among the best known are : " Is He Yours ? " " No

Burdens Yonder," "He Will Hold Me Fast," "Christ Needs You," "Bearing the Cross," "Shadows," "Oh, What a Change," "Does Jesus Care?" "The Crown of Thorns," "The Joy Awaiting," etc.

"How do you write your hymns, Mr. Harkness?" asked an interviewer.

"How do I write them?" returned the composer. "Why, I write them when I've got them, and when I haven't got them I don't write. You can't write what you haven't got, you know. Of course, my work varies. Perhaps I will write the music to thirty hymns in one day, then again I may not write but one a month. It depends upon the inspiration. I get my inspiration from incidents. When at the piano at an evangelistic service I keep a note-book and pencil handy, and as the service proceeds some suggestion for a hymn may come to me, possibly several suggestions. These I jot down for reference later. Perhaps in these there is the suggestion for the melody to a hymn. I get a melody in my mind and then I sit down to the piano and play it; if it pleases me I write it down and examine it afterwards."

Mr. Harkness in company with Mr. Alexander has belted the globe. While in the United States, as well as in Europe, he visited many cities, serving as accompanist in the great Torrey–Alexander and Chapman–Alexander meetings—and everywhere was royally received.

Mr. Harkness commented in an interesting way on the method of making the song service in these great meetings successful. The weather has much to do with his adjusting the music to the assembled company. If it is a stormy night the voices of the people as a rule have not got the range that they have on a crisp cold night. In the first instance they will not sing as high as on a cold night. In the morning the voice is lower in range. He explained that if he played in the same key morning and evening, the singing would not be the success that it should be. In the morning the audience will sing up to D, while in the evening it will sing up to F.

"If church organists would watch this to keep the music of the hymns within the range of the voices of the people of the audience they would have better singing, and therefore a better tone to the service. In a small hall, or one where the ceiling is low, it is also necessary to keep the voices down as regards the range, otherwise what would sound well in a large hall would sound like screeching."

Mr. Harkness at present is living in London, England, where he is composing gospel songs for Mr. Alexander.

It is not the belief of the writer that this musical genius was found in that far-away country by mere chance by Mr. Alexander. Undoubtedly the Lord was leader and guide.

> " In all thy ways acknowledge Him, and
> He shall direct thy paths."
> —*Proverbs iii. 6.*

> " For this God is our God forever and ever :
> He will be our guide even unto death."
> —*Psalm xlviii. 14.*

May Mr. Harkness live long and continue to use his heaven-born gifts in the ministry of gospel song to bless the world and to God's glory.

Printed in the United States of America